£9.95

D0518501

A PLANTSMAN'S PERSPECTIVE

A PLANTSMAN'S PERSPECTIVE

Alan Bloom

Plants, people and places

COLLINS
8 Grafton Street, London W1X 3LA

First published in 1987 by
William Collins Sons and Co Ltd
London · Glasgow · Sydney · Auckland · Toronto
Johannesburg

Jacket photograph by Marianne Majerus

Edited by Robert Pearson

British Library Cataloguing in Publication Data
Bloom, Alan, *1906–*
    A plantsman's perspective.
    1. Gardening
    I. Title
    635'.092'4   SB455

    ISBN 0 00 412262 3

Printed and bound in Great Britain by
Robert Hartnoll (1985) Ltd, Bodmin

Contents

Introduction

This book was begun not as a preconceived plan, but on an impulse. I had just entered my 80th year, which comes, for most of us who reach it, as a reminder that it is indeed later than we thought. Inevitably, we think of times past, of people we knew, of wrong turnings and opportunities lost as well as the changes we have lived to see. For me, all these facets and more tend to put past years in perspective, and, in the process, what I have been able to achieve on the credit side becomes a cause for thankfulness rather than for pride.

Most of the chapters deal with a single subject, as a result of either stirring up memories or putting on paper thoughts which from time to time have come into my head while at work – which I had never previously considered recording. That others might some day find them of interest was the spur.

As a miscellany, the subjects range from water, so vital to growth, to weeds, which are the gardener's constant adversary. Another chapter records, mostly with affection, gardeners whose devotion I admired, along with a few I came to shun. In case someone might be interested I wrote a potted history of my endeavours as a young nurseryman, a nursery which sixty years later my sons have developed into one of the foremost in Europe. Deviations into farming and land reclamation, to making a lake and becoming a backwoodsman in Canada, are recorded along with the making of a five-acre garden in which to grow plants for love rather than for profit.

Visitors sometimes ask what are my favourite flowers – a question I can never answer shortly but have now done at length. My opinions at the age of twenty on this and that were much more rigid than when old age knocked at my door. But a few which have stood the test of time are scattered here and there, as are some views which, in my brash immaturity, were beyond contemplation – or comprehension. One has to live in order to learn. One has to experience the harsh aspects of life in order to appreciate what brings joy or peace of mind. Through my inconstancies, there has, thankfully, been a zest for work along with an abiding, constant love of plants and of nature.

To be known as a plantsman is to me an honour, and what I have written attempts to put my life, chequered though it is, in perspective.

Alan Bloom

CHAPTER ONE

Early Days in a Different World

The nursery trade has undergone some profound changes since 1940. So have many other industries, one might say, but I very much doubt if a comparison could be made if only because nurseries are probably the least adaptable of any commercial venture to mechanisation. The majority of garden-minded people can have little idea of what conditions were like before World War II, and, rather than quote facts and figures, it may be of interest to know how different it was then for one who began sixty-five years ago as a sixteen-year-old learner.

I left high school fed up with authority and wanting only to begin working with plants. My parents were then, in July 1922, on the point of moving from Over to Oakington, half way to Cambridge, to take over a six-acre holding on much lighter soil. But being a market grower, Father believed I should work on a proper nursery as a learner and off we went to Wisbech. The largest firm there specialising in perennials was R.H. Bath Ltd, but they said they had no vacancy for me. We then went to find G.W. Miller and Son of Clarkson Nurseries and there sat the white-bearded Mr Miller himself dividing heuchera plants. Quite gruffly and with very few words he offered to take me on at ten shillings for a week of fifty-two hours, and he would fix up lodgings for me.

I stayed in those lodgings for only one night, for they proved to be no more than a lodging house. I'd been assigned a top floor room in which were two double beds and one single. Their occupants came up to bed belching and swearing long after me. I lay wedged between one of them and the wall, scarcely sleeping at all. Next morning I told Harry Giles, with whom I'd been put to work, how rough the lodgings were, and, taking pity on me, he offered to let me move into his house that same evening. But day after day the work was planting in narrow beds or weeding. The variety of jobs I was given to do was very limited, and only the most menial ones came my way. Ten weeks later I was back home vowing never to leave again. But my parents wisely saw to it that I did, and looking back I realize they must have found my brashness somewhat intolerable.

An uncle living close to Wallace's nursery at Tunbridge Wells, Kent arranged for me to go there as a learner. There I learned how to wash and crock pots, barrow and mix soil, to remove and move back 200 6 ft by 4 ft frame lights night and morning, and be at the beck and call of my superiors in the potting shed whenever they wanted errands carried out. The nursery was known as 'The Old Gardens' and had a central roadway flanked mainly by shrubs, including a selection of large rhododendrons, some of which had been lifted for the Wembley Exhibition. On one errand I met the great Mr Wallace himself, who even gave me a nod, though not a friendly one. Later that day, as a result of a reprimand coming down from Mr Wallace through the manager, Mr Hughes, my foreman, Mr Reeves, told me that I must never again walk about with my hands behind my back. It was Mr Wallace's sole privilege so to do, as it was his privilege also to conduct the titled or wealthy visitors who were his best customers. The second class of customer was for Mr Hughes as manager, and third class customers were in a foreman's charge, especially those who wished to select and take away pot-grown plants. Otherwise, orders were booked for delivery in season. And in season, boxes full of lily bulbs – a Wallace speciality –arrived from Japan, crates of bulbs and perennials from Holland, trees and shrubs from English wholesale nurseries packed in huge bundles tied in with straw or sacking. Some Dutch stock came in large wicker hampers, the tops of azaleas, rhododendrons and so on protected by a conical tent-like structure.

I was paid 15 shillings a week at Wallace's. Cheekily, I asked for a rise after a few months and was awarded another half crown. But not being allowed to pot or propagate plants I was dissatisfied and, after six months, found a vacancy at Arthur Charlton's nursery on the Eridge Road. It was a long, narrow nursery beside a railway embankment, and I was put in charge of the rock and alpine plants, a small department of a general nursery which included perennials and indoor plants. The larger shrub nursery was a few miles away at Rotherfield. My weekly wage had jumped to 30 shillings and at last I was able to save a few shillings after paying my landlady, whose husband was a wheel tapper on the railway. Alpines were, of course, grown in clay pots and plunged in ashes, but being allocated a little greenhouse I was able to propagate both alpines and perennials and to raise seeds. My boss was John Charlton who not only taught me several things I did not know, but was remarkably tolerant of mistakes I made in my ignorance.

The perennials were grown in the then standard narrow beds which measured six feet across. One had to be very neat and meticulous to ensure straight edges, padded with a spade to each intersecting two-foot path. White-painted wooden labels were used with the names written in pencil while the paint was still wet, this paint being rubbed on with a finger rather than a brush. Not many customers came direct to the nursery to buy plants, but many were sold at the firm's shop in The Pantiles, Tunbridge Wells. Most open ground plants were sold in autumn and spring for use in landscaping contracts and deliveries were made both by a Ford van and a curious steam lorry which had a transverse boiler in front.

After a year at Charlton's I had an urge to go north and a trip on the new 'Flying Scotsman' to York ended with a post at Longster's Nursery at Malton. But promises of encouragement to work-up stocks of alpines and perennials were not kept, and despite a high wage for an eighteen-year-old of £2 per week, I moved after only six weeks to R. V. Rogers nursery at Pickering, a few miles further north, to take the job of propagator for 36 shillings. This was a go-ahead, expanding general nursery under the constant drive and guidance of Mr Roger, a tall, handsome man who was always in a hurry. Here there was every encouragement to work and to learn as fast as I could, and, with a younger boy, Tom Fletcher, to help me we produced results which pleased Mr Roger, but not the foreman who had previously been propagator as well.

Sid Fasoms was my superior, and, having worked for the legendary Reginald Farrer, he considered himself to be an expert on alpines. As such he was critical of me, especially when inspecting the contents of

my propagating glasshouse. It came to a head one day when my
resentment of what I saw as unjustified interference boiled over. I was
heftier than he was and ordered him out, advancing menacingly
towards him. I had no intention of being violent but he retreated and
went straight to Mr Roger. Soon Mr Roger came striding along to give
me a somewhat paternal lecture on keeping the peace. It impressed me
and seemed to establish a mutual respect and friendship which lasted
until he died forty years later. Sid Fasoms never bothered me again and
when I left to begin working on my own speciality with my father at
Oakington, I had begun to realise I had still a long way to go to be a
successful nurseryman. There had been times when, inspired by the
books of Farrer and Kingdon Ward, I hankered to become a plant
hunter in far off places. But when I learned that several years training
as a botanist would be a prerequisite, the notion melted away in favour
of becoming a master nurseryman.

Although tractors were coming into wider use on the farms in the
1920s, nurseries had no other means of power than men and horses.
We had three men and one horse in 1926. Flowers for cutting were
grown in long rows, and the horse was used for inter-row cultivation,
carting soil, sand and manure and taking the produce to the local
railway station for dispatch to distant markets. It also went between
the shafts of the buggy when private journeys were made, but with a
propensity for bolting it could never be left untethered between the
shafts of the buggy or the nursery trolley. Wheelbarrows and hand
trucks were, of course, manhandled, and, with no mains water supply,
watering other than from the greenhouse rain water tank necessitated
manual pumping from a well when using the hosepipe.

I longed to be able to put up exhibits at flower shows, but to take
flowers and plants by rail was too costly and complicated, though
some nurserymen still used this means of transport. I had put up
exhibits at a few shows for Mr Roger and believed this was the only
way to become established – by taking orders for later despatch.
Wholesale business also appealed to me, and once a few kinds of plants
were available a classified advertisement in the *Horticultural Trades
Journal* would usually meet with some response. I also sent out a typed
list – four copies at a time on an ancient machine – to any firm I
thought might be in need of any of the hundred or so items offered.

There were at that time at least a dozen specialists in perennials and alpines and many more, like Wallace's and Charlton's, who included them as a section of a general nursery.

By 1927, however, I had persuaded father that motor transport was vital. But a new vehicle was beyond his means, and when I found a 1920 Austin 20 h.p. tourer for £25 he and Herbert Smith converted it into a van. It was not a success – but this was my fault rather than theirs as I was the driver. When it ran it was extravagant but more often it refused to run at all, and it was discarded in favour of a new Trojan van on hire purchase. This cost £140 on solid tyres and its two-stroke engine under the seat was capable of 30 m.p.h. In it I took and staged exhibits at Southport, Leeds, York, Cheltenham and several other shows nearer home. It was also used to take produce to sell on local market stalls as well as hawking plants around the residential districts of Cambridge. Much effort for minimal returns was disheartening and all day spent at Cambridge market on my twenty-first birthday brought sales of only twenty-six shillings.

In 1929 my younger brother George came into the business and took over the Trojan and direct sales much to my relief, for I was a poor salesman and chafed to spend more time with plants. We both went to Southport Show that August. But apart from putting up a mixture of flowering perennials and alpines and taking more orders than usual, we nursed a secret scheme to include several boxes of everlasting statice to offer when selling off-time came at the end. Father had sent these by rail and we hid them under the table exhibit knowing it was strictly against the rules (only what had been exhibited was supposed to be sold). The need arose from a glutted market for cut flowers, and the bunches at sixpence a time were going well when the show secretary bore down angrily and put a stop to it. The penalty was to be banned from exhibiting there ever again – at a period when Southport was a better show than Chelsea for business. Total sales that year were only £779.

Business became decidedly slack over the next year or two of depression. And when my parents and brother moved to Mildenhall in 1930 we had to share the same bank account and I had to keep within a £50 overdraft. The wages of my three helpers, two men and a lad, totalled only £4 per week while my new wife managed on £2 weekly with which to keep house. It was quite tough but the total takings from the now fifteen-acre holding only just exceeded £1,000 for the first time in 1931. As stocks and orders of plants for sale slowly increased, so the market-growing side diminished.

There were only two glasshouses at Oakington and not very large ones at that. But although there was a local outlet for tomatoes in summer, I carried on with pot plants under glass for winter and spring. Twice weekly I did a round of Cambridge shops with azaleas, cyclamen, lily-of-the-valley, primulas, and so on, in keeping with my preference for wholesaling. One or two shops also took alpines in pots on sale or return at 3s6d per dozen, but, as the business became more specialised in outdoor plants, I was glad to drop the indoor production. The azaleas, by the way, all came from Belgium, and although roots often had to be chopped to entice them into pots, they never suffered so long as ample water was given them.

Much the same attitude towards wholesaling encouraged sales to firms who were already specialists in perennials and alpines. This was on the understanding that if I became strictly wholesale only, they, too, would be more likely to buy what they needed from me knowing that I was not competing for their retail outlets. Such firms, or indeed any who grew primarily for retail, only offered surpluses to the trade and then only in spring when such surpluses became apparent. Either they would send out a trade list or advertise in one of the three trade journals. Classified advertisements in these journals had been my means of increasing orders and was still a regular practice even when my range of plants increased sufficiently to warrant an annual trade catalogue. Not that this compared for variety with such firms as Perry, Prichard, Wells, Artindale, Bees, Bakers of Codsall, Gayborder and others who were at the top during the early 1930s.

Variety as well as quality spurred my ambitions. At that time the basic wholesale price for both pot-grown alpines and field-grown perennials was 3s6d per dozen, and 25s per 100, carriage paid for cash with order. This price was for easily grown plants, and those in greater demand and those which took more time and trouble to produce went up in steps from 28s per 100 to 50s per 100 for such items as paeonias. Similarly, retail prices were from 6d per plant, with 9d more general, up to 2s for such plants as paeonias or named delphiniums. The latter were much in vogue then, mostly as a result of Blackmore and Langdon's developments. For me they were a prestige range to grow and offer, but proved unprofitable because of over-anxiety to produce them in quantity. Losses came from both over-propagation and disease, I having made the mistake of trying to force new growth under glass by a method suggested by Sir Roland Biffen, the then Director of the National Institute of Agricultural Botany at Cambridge.

Going wholesale only, after my last exhibit at Chelsea Show in 1934, came as a kind of relief and stimulant. I was not a good salesman in the verbal sense and chafed at the time away when I could have been better and more congenially employed at home. By that year plant growing had almost ousted market flower growing and not much of the nine-acre meadow adjoining was left. My parents had bought it for £600 in 1928 and for the first two or three winters we dug it by hand, little by little. I could not disagree with Father's belief that this was the best method. It was good deep soil and the turf was spaded off to be covered by at least a foot of soil. Such trenching was inevitably slow work, and finding Saxon skeletons and a shield seemed to prove that it had not been cultivated for over a thousand years. But a little arithmetic when, in 1931, I was in sole control, showed how costly hand digging was, and the rest, thereafter, was ploughed by horses as required. Apart from the cost of digging, the subsequent cropping was poor because the buried turf shrank to leave root-inhibiting cavities.

My parents had been generous. The prevailing interest rate was five per cent and this was the figure in which the rent was based for the house and fifteen acres. What stock there was left when they moved to Mildenhall was at my valuation and was paid off by instalments. They had unselfishly given way to my ambitions even though Father preferred glasshouse to outdoor crops, and family relations became closer as a result. My unruly tendencies must have brought them anxieties in past years, but having given me this freedom, the new situation had brought mutual benefits and I was glad to be able to pay back their investment in me by degrees.

By 1936 I was looking for more land, buoyed up by success. It was especially pleasing that nurserymen who had been buying perennials from Holland were now finding Oakington plants were as good or better, and if I, too, was buying from Holland, this was for purely stock-building purposes in terms of variety and quantity. Every year the Dutchmen came over for several weeks at a time canvassing orders for all kinds of nursery stock, but although the 1931 ten per cent protective duty on such imports imposed by our government had been helpful to British producers, vast quantities were still coming over.

But if I was much preoccupied with the business there was still time for recreation and social life, tennis and fishing in summer, skating and card playing in winter. By day it was mostly work of a kind too enjoyable to miss, merely ordering others to do my bidding. With so much on my doorstep in respect of new plants to care for, I had virtually no private garden. Not being a retail nursery there were no incoming customers apart from a few in the nursery trade wanting to order or take away plants. I scarcely needed a private garden in which to grow special plants, for they were close at hand under daily surveillance. If sand was needed I liked to dig a pit myself, and the wells, too, when more spread of irrigation was required. When wet patches showed up in a rainy spell I enjoyed digging trenches and laying pipe drains, and when I found a low spot into which drains could flow, I joined in digging out a pond to make it an ornamental sump. And it all had to be done by hand, dumping the spoil into what ten years before had been the 'Boggery' referred to in Chapter Two, 'Wet and Dry'.

By 1937 there were over thirty acres of plants with half a million alpines in pots and over thirty helpers. No longer was it my job alone to pot, plant, invoice and take stock, compile a catalogue and do the book-keeping as it had been for most of the past ten years. And I was coming to realise how fortunate I had been in having the loyal, devoted help of three unrelated Smiths. There was Herbert, a man of my father's age, who came to tell us in 1926 that we needed him as much as he wanted to work on a nursery. He could be irascible and short tempered with slackers when they failed to come up to the example he set for hard work. To me he was forthright in his opinions and generous in his advice, as if I had been the son he never had. As a skilled all-rounder with tools he taught me much and I came to admire and respect his utter reliability.

Then there was Len Smith whose mother came on washdays as well as to cut and bunch flowers for market. Len came to help me at any free time even before he left school, and became nicknamed 'Lightning' for his alacrity. This association also began in 1926. In those early days I would pot alpines and he plunged them in sand, and competition became the rule, but only when potting rooted cuttings was easy could I match his speed at plunging. He was taught by his mother to call me 'Master Alan' and never lost the habit, even when, forty years later, he was manager of a large nursery near St. Albans. At Oakington by 1937 he was in charge of alpines and propagating, to become overall manager when Herbert Smith retired and I moved to Fordham to be nearer the farm in Burwell Fen (see p.20).

Then there was Ethel Smith, a forty-year-old spinster when she came from London to live with her sister at Oakington in 1935. Of rather gaunt but superior appearance, Ethel took over the office work following a break-up of her London job, and as she regained her equanimity began to ask for more work to be given her. Herbert Smith built her a wooden office enabling her to move out of the room in my house which had served until then. Her coming was timely and her devotion complete, to the extent that she was not afraid to remind me of the duties which I should be performing but which she took on gladly to relieve me. Both she and her sister Winifred, denied marriage as a result of the war, were trusty friends when domestic troubles came my way over the next few years. It is one of my lasting regrets that I had to hurt them by declining their wish to move to Bressingham when the Oakington property was vacated in 1947. Ethel and Len Smith had managed this during much of the war period with only weekly visits from me.

During the early weeks and months after September 3, 1939 there was virtually no demand for plants. Everyone expected immediate bombings with gas attacks and other horrors. That nothing happened until the summer of 1940 made no difference to trade stagnation. It was saddening to walk round the nursery and to realise that all those plants were now of practically no market value. No one would even be willing to have them free for the taking, and when the expected direction to switch over to food crops came, most of them had to be ploughed under. It was a sad irony, too, that having just achieved my ambition to be master of a hardy plant nursery equal in essentials to the best in the country, it had become as valueless as a burst balloon as far as future prospects were concerned. The challenge had vanished along with the successes and the failures from which I had learned. Of course, there had been warnings as Hitler's threats took shape, but, like most other people, I fostered hopes that war would be averted. I even wrote letters to 28 German nurserymen advocating peace weeks before war was declared, but none responded and no doubt the letters were intercepted.

Oakington was now on the edge of an RAF bomber station and as Head Air Raid Warden with a siren on my house there were fears for my three infant children. By 1940 I was their only parent. But for the devotion to them of two other Smiths, a mother and daughter who were housekeeper and nanny, I would have been even more fearful and frustrated now that my Burwell farm, twenty miles away, had to take up far more of my time than the nursery. But at least there were challenges and duties to take the edge of anxieties and there was the constant support of staunch friends – most of them Smiths.

CHAPTER TWO

Wet and Dry

It is in the nature of some people to have to learn the hard way. They may read books designed to give advice on various aspects of gardening, yet somehow fail to digest or remember what they read. There again, situations occur and improvements suggest themselves which are not included specifically in any gardening books. Or more likely, as with me, an idea has occurred which brings with it an impulsive urge to tackle it right away, because it offered a new and exciting interest. I recall my first attempt to grow plants where none had ever grown before, of kinds that I had never before been able to grow. I was in my late teens – the age at which some people believe they know all they need to know for success in life. My parents had recently bought a nine-acre meadow adjoining their five-acre nursery near Cambridge, and, having returned from gaining some experience on other nurseries I had decided to become a specialist in perennials and alpines rather than follow my father's bent for growing flowers and fruit on a market garden. This struck me as too restrictive, too hazardous, giving too little opportunity to propagate, to collect and grow a wide variety of plants.

There was a ditch on the far side of the meadow in which water ran in lesser or greater quantities for most of the year. On the far side, elm trees shaded the ditch for much of the day, and, if the nearside bank was steep and grew only nettles and sheep's parsley, there was one place where it was gently sloping, like a cut-away bay. This, obviously, had been a drinking place for cattle, but now it was a patch of mud about five yards across, a foot or two above the water level in the ditch. Ideal, I believed, for a place in which to grow bog plants – primulas, calthas and the like, for which no other site was suitable. All it grew now, in that spring of 1927, was a few docks and creeping buttercups.

Digging to make a tilth was more than difficult. The mud had congealed, but no matter – bog plants need boggy conditions surely, and to ensure constant moisture I made a little channel around what my mother had dubbed the 'Boggery'. Into this ditch water was encouraged to flow by means of a low dam of clayey lumps flattened down in the ditch itself. Planting followed, as did the first misgivings, because, instead of the hoped for tilth, the surface was now crusty lumps which refused to break down. May having come, it was too late to buy in additions to the three or four kinds of moisture-loving kinds I had already. I had sown seeds of others but it was too soon to plant the few which had germinated. But by July it was clear that what I had already planted were dying and a fresh crop of seedling docks and creeping buttercups were intent on taking over. The Boggery was a dismal failure, and if I caught a glimpse of the reason, other ventures had to come before I fully grasped the need most plants have for easy root penetration. Moisture, vital as it is, is only one requirement of moisture-loving plants.

Some years later, in 1938, I became the proud owner of a 200-acre farm deep in the peaty fens at Burwell. Its purchase at what might now seem a ridiculously low price of £1,600 had been made possible by a lucky venture into the then new Korean chrysanthemums which yielded just that amount of profit. Apart from a hankering to be a farmer as well as a nurseryman, a main objective was to compete with Dutch producers of perennials who had collared a large share of the British wholesale trade. The Burwell soil was not unlike that of Holland's famed nursery area, Boskoop. It was poorly drained but I was keen enough to imagine it to be possible to overcome such a disability. In the previous year I had hired a field in a neighbouring fen as an experiment, planting four acres with quite a wide variety of plants. But within a week or two all were inundated by a March flood which left the soil surface caked, and, although it was stirred again between the rows when sufficiently dry, the plants failed to take root and compete with the annual weeds which flourished lustily.

Not a fair trial, I thought, as we later transferred the surviving plants into a field in Burwell Fen, which I reckoned was least likely to become waterlogged. Apart from needing to be kept free of fat hen, willow weed and chickweed, plant growth was reasonably good. But hopes of being able to sell the plants dwindled as that summer of 1939 drew on towards harvest time, with the certainty that for the foreseeable grim, dim future, both the Burwell Farm and the Oakington nursery of 36 acres would have to concentrate on food crops. Not even a 25 per cent reduction overall on the 1,870 items in my catalogue that autumn brought more than a quarter of the normal orders and the plants at Burwell were ploughed under.

The drainage problem, however, remained. Some fields had cropped poorly because of inadequate dykes and the inefficiency of the district drainage system. The main drain to the pumping station ran beside an embanked Lode with a ten-foot difference in water levels. Water leaked from the Lode into the main drain so choked that as soon as the pump stopped – as it often did – water ran back into the subsidiary dykes. I contrived a kind of sluice to prevent this happening, with a wooden flap which was intended to open when the pump – a mile or more away – was working and to close when the flow went into reverse. It failed to operate unless someone was there to push the flap into position at the correct time. But when the district pump failed completely and irrevocably, the overall Authority took over and within a year or two the Burwell system was merged to become part of a larger scheme. This led to me taking on another 300 acres of adjoining land which had become abandoned and derelict. Reeds and bushes had taken over when peat digging for fuel ceased to be profitable years before. To reclaim it for food production was, in part, at least, a form of sublimation for the decimation of my nursery output of perennials for the duration of the war.

That seven years' experience, in which drainage played a vital part, should have been enough to put me off tackling land liable to become waterlogged. There were imperative reasons for getting out of both the Burwell and Oakington holdings, but water still held a fascination for me. I turned down a very good offer to take over a 300-acre farm on light land because it had no stream. But when my search for a farm led me to Bressingham, near Diss in Norfolk, the challenge it presented was too great to resist. The land sloped gently down to the infant Waveney river, and half the 220 acres of the farm was black, fenny and neglected. It was surprising that almost all this valley bottom had escaped the wartime dictates of clearing and cropping, implying, as it did, that the Norfolk 'War Ag.' had not been as thorough as that of Cambridgeshire. It was the occupying vendor's statement that the river was to be deepened by three feet which did away with my misgivings, coupled with such factors as an attractive looking house, a wealth of trees and the rest of the land being about right for both farming and nursery work. And that it would be easy to make the low land productive, compared with what I had tackled in Burwell Fen.

In the event, the river was scarcely deepened at all. Some official had failed to survey it beforehand and in parts the course was not in the lowest part of the valley, as was made very evident when a flood came at the end of that grim winter of 1947, covering the valley up to two feet deep in water. Even fields above flood level were so sodden that trenches had to be dug and pipe drains laid before the nursery stock from Oakington could be planted. These loamy fields which had appeared so kind and workable the year before were anything but kindly now, and, with the arrival of drying winds, soapy looking lumps turned into hard clods as the cold, wet spring turned to parching summer. Irrigation became essential only a few weeks after saturation, to give more than a hint that I still had much to learn about the relationship between soil and water. I was still learning the hard way and here it seemed that the soil, while sound as a growing medium, lacked some structural quality causing it to congeal with excessive moisture. There could be no other reason why those acres of plants failed that year to make new roots quickly, and allowed drought to stunt the growth of those that survived.

Irrigation was helpful in keeping plants alive in such conditions, or would have been had there been clean water for the spray lines. These lines had been very successful on the light Oakington soil, the water being pumped from wells I had enjoyed digging to find an abundant supply only fifteen feet below in the gravel. But here at Bressingham there was no water-bearing gravel, and, because of delays in obtaining a permit to buy steel tubing, water had to be pumped from a fen ditch until we gave up trying to keep the spray nozzles clear of algae. When at last the steel tubing came and was driven first through three feet of soft sand, then through sixty feet of clay and another fifty feet of chalk, water the colour of milk came up with pumping. After several hours it slowly became clear, and, as the pump was stopped, it welled up to the surface clear and cold.

The sight of it, suffering as I was along with my plants stricken by drought, brought tears of relief. There followed several happy hours making rivulets with water from the new artesian well into the one fen field we had been able to plant. This was a primitive method of irrigation, but with water mains and branches still to be laid, it was a quick life-saver for several thousand young phlox – as well as a throw-back to boyhood when I used to make little dams and waterfalls just for fun whenever the opportunity occured. But a year later I was preparing to go to Canada as an emigrant with my young family. Frustrations of many kinds had dogged me since coming to Bressingham and the idea of pioneering in a freer land was also a hangover from boyhood. But British Columbia was not after all a land of opportunity for such as me, and when, in desperation, I bought six acres of recently logged-out forest with a cabin-type house on the sea front, it was not long before I realised I had again been somewhat impulsive. There was very little land clear of stumps, rotting timber and saplings on which to dig a garden. Where it was not boggy there was a hard pan, and to dig a garden patch meant digging ditches first, using a pick to break up the hard pan beneath.

The worst winter for thirty years on Vancouver Island ended with me having to take on piece-work for a new road, felling and burning trees, until I realised I could never make a living there in the wilds. Back halfway to England on a small run-down holding in Ontario I guessed the prospects would be brighter, but within two weeks a well which the vendor said had never run dry did so, and most of the summer of 1949 was spent digging for water. After test holes and a twenty-five-foot deep well (where a dowser had said there were oodles of water) it eventually came as a result of a 700 ft long pipe which I laid three and a half feet deep from a spring on a neighbour's property. But when early in 1950, came news of mismanagement and financial straits at Bressingham there was no other course than to go back to grapple with the problems from which I should never have run away.

Being well and truly chastened, we arrived back at Bressingham in March 1950 and, having summarily dismissed the offending management and obtained a hefty bank loan, my first and foremost priority was to restore the nursery business. The problem of the soil's water content had to take second place in the knowledge that trouble would recur soon enough. Thirty-six years have passed since then, and because the drainage authority have still not made the Waveney capable of taking all the water away without flooding the adjoining land, the threat of loss is ever-present during wet periods. Severe losses have occurred on three or four occasions as rain water from the wide catchment area is held up by the bottle-necked river a little down-stream of our land. Even saturation, causing consolidation of the black, fenny soil of the valley, will inhibit growth. In the early days it struck me as very strange to see puddles on the land when only a few yards away was a ditch with its water level three feet or more below the surface. One would have expected puddles to quickly soak away through such easy-working soil, but even one's footmark in freshly stirred land would hold water from subsequent rainfall.

Some fen fields were uneven as a result of past erosion from the uplands bringing down fine sand and clay. This process must have taken centuries and left low mounds or banks of sand between which marsh vegetation, as it decayed, built up the peat. Culvitation lowered the peat level through shrinkage and so left the sand a foot or two higher. In the belief that more sand mixed with the peat would improve both fertility and drainage, sand was dug out from the banks and spread on to the low peaty places. I also made a two-acre lake on the edge of the fen and a few thousand cubic yards of sand and clayey subsoil were spread over the two nearest fen fields. This improved the texture, but it did not improve drainage. The mixture was still prone to consolidate in wet periods. Then it slowly began to dawn on me that the fine soft sand was itself a main cause for the problem, added to the most erratic and unreliable water table, due to the inadequate river outfall.

It was very odd, I thought, that where quite heavy clay soil, almost free of sand, was under cultivation drainage was less of a problem. Soil structure was no problem at all for the first two or three years when making a large garden near my house. It had probably been meadow for generations and although there was no great depth of soil, the chopped-up turf dug in gave new plantings a good start. The subsoil was a mixture of clay and sand, the clay being basic, and after a few years consolidation again became a worry. It did not occur to me to consult a soil expert but only to use my own judgement based on experience of several types of soil. Peat was dug in but contrary to my hopes and expectations it was no remedy and there was little evidence that plant roots made use of it, nor to any extent was compost and farm manure of noticcable benefit. When replanting after a few years and digging the ground as deeply as when it was first converted from grass, it came up with a sour smell, congealed by the pressure from above – people's feet and by weekly overhead irrigation during dry periods.

It had often puzzled me why some plants such as the leafy ligularias were drooping under sun and wind when they had received a good watering maybe only the day before. Examination of the soil to the depth of a fork showed that indeed it was not dry, and I could only put it down to sun and wind affecting the foliage, especially as by morning growth was again turgid. It was a visit to Maurice Mason's Norfolk garden at Larchwood which gave a clue to what I should have realised long before. The visit was during a quite severe drought, but there, at Larchwood, were groups of ligularias, hostas and the like growing on light, stony soil in open spaces between a great variety of mature trees, and showing no signs at all of flagging. There could be only one explanation. Both top and subsoil was far more open than in my garden and root penetration was easy down to where it was naturally or more permanently moist. Maybe some shade and protection from strong winds was a contributory factor, but bang went my long-standing belief that a clay-based soil with sand in with the top layer was ideal for plant growth.

It stands out starkly for me, after sixty-five years as a cultivator, that I have paid too little attention to soil structures. Lack of moisture and seeing plants suffer in a drought has always been distressing to me. This was probably the reason for the urge to irrigate by some means or other, and, although fully aware of the need to keep a surface tilth amongst growing plants in dry weather, my attraction to soil moisture became something of a fixation and led to other factors such as soil structure and root penetration being overlooked until quite recent years. At Oakington there were two distinct types of soil on the fifteen acres I owned and a third type on a field I rented. Four acres were of deep, light soil over gravel. It dried out quickly, but plants made better growth on this soil than on the rest, which was good-looking brown loam over greensand, below which was blue clay. The greensand was not free draining and one had to be careful not to work on it while it was damp. This latter precaution applied even more to the rented field which was heavy with clay close to the surface. On none of these was it possible to dig with a spade because it would not keep itself clean. This was due to a lack of sand, for at Bressingham almost anywhere a spade will work cleanly, although it is hard work where soil is panned down or dry.

My own preference when digging is always for a fork. Tines penetrate more freely than a blade and if the soil is heavy lumps can more easily be broken down. A fork gives more choice in the kind of dug surface one wishes to leave – rough and lumpy for frost to break down or fine for early planting. If there are perennial weeds such as couch, a fork is far more effective in shaking it out, whereas a spade will chop them into smaller pieces, any of which left below the surface will grow again. Generally, a fork will penetrate more deeply than a spade and it is also a better tool when adding manure or compost at the time of digging.

Reverting to the problem of soil structure, the long-term remedy came as a result of an experiment. In trying to figure out why the fine particles of sand on much of the Bressingham soil did nothing to improve drainage and structure, it occurred to me when peat and compost both failed to try coarse, sharp sand. When replanting groups of plants where the soil was most congealed, half an inch or so of the sand was spread over and dug in – with a fork, of course. There was a marked improvement in plant growth and even more so wherever a second application at a later date also had the effect of mixing it more thoroughly. Over the eight years since that first experiment a lorry load of sharp sand is dumped once a year at each end of the five-acre garden – and more for my little nursery field nearby. By late spring it has all gone into the soil and year by year the improvement shows up increasingly. The beneficial results bring me no pride, for had I been more assiduously observant this method of soil improvement would have been used long before.

Instead of pride come reflections that many of the losses – indicated by a box full of labels in the tool shed relating no longer to plants which have a place in the garden – have been due to the poor soil structure I failed to remedy. And it is galling to reflect, too, that some of these plants were partial to moisture, indicating, as it does, that even bog primulas thrive best where their roots can freely penetrate the soil. Hostas, the sturdy kinds at least, are more adaptable and I once found traces of their roots four feet down. In a general way it seems that the more fibrous-rooted plants are in greatest need for an open soil, with no lack of humus and sharp sand – whether or not they are moisture lovers. There is, however, no general rule, for such fleshy rooted plants as dicentras, verbascums and eryngiums cannot abide tight, damp soil, and while the fibrous-rooted astilbes, trilliums and trollius dislike a dryish, light medium, the primrose type of *Primula* are happy in stiff clay. One lives and learns but none of us live long enough to learn more than a portion of what makes for perfection.

There are places in Britain where soil lacks stability – where the sand content is so great that it would benefit from added clay to give it more body. Both the Norfolk Brecklands and the Woking-Bagshot area of Surrey, including The Royal Horticultural Society's Wisley Garden, have problems in this respect. As a tailpiece, however, there is a sad story to tell of a new garden I planted in Ireland. Its owner, whose name I'll change to Patrick, had built a new hotel beside a main road well to the west of Dublin. Having read one of my books he came over to see my garden and invited me to visit his property and plan one for him. The site sloped gently away from the smart new hotel down to a stream. Near the stream the soil was damp and peaty, just right for beds of moisture-loving perennials, while, round the hotel itself, there was ample scope for a wide range of perennials, conifers and alpines which would be happy on a bank beside the car park. There was an obvious need to ensure that the peaty area was drained into the nearby stream, which, in wet periods, would raise the water table to cause trouble.

With an assurance that pipes would be laid, I pegged out island beds in consultation with Patrick, whose enthusiasm made up for his lack of knowledge to a large extent. The beds and borders would, he said, be well dug and prepared by the time I returned in the autumn of 1978 to take a lead in planting. The lorry load of planting material arrived a day ahead of my own arrival with the prospect of an enjoyable week's break, staying as a hotel guest. But it was not to be. Three of the peaty island beds were not fit to plant and others had been poorly prepared. Footmarks squelched, with other indications that no drainage work had been done. Patrick explained that after all he had not thought it necessary, especially as the weather had been dry when the digging was done and that drainage pipes and skilled workers had not been found.

But at least Patrick helped me to dig little trenches to drain water from the beds towards the stream. Having done so, I laid out and planted up the drier places, to finish up with the peaty beds – unluckily in pouring rain – and returned home after eight days of quite intensive activity with a little help now and then from Patrick. I could but impress on him the need to properly drain those waterlogged beds without further delay. I doubt if he ever did, or ever put permanent labels to the 300 kinds of plants he now possessed. He paid up promptly and I heard no more from him. But from a gardening friend who stayed at the hotel three years later, I learned that for some reason Patrick had apparently lost interest, and, when neglect became a bad advertisement, the beds were put down to grass and only the conifers remained of what had cost much in time, effort and money.

CHAPTER THREE

More Ups and Downs

Onions, carrots and outdoor tomatoes were already ousting perennials by the summer of 1940. The Dunkirk spirit, backed by Churchill's speeches, inspired most people to think of Britain as the Island Fortress – beginning for me, of course, at home with three children under five. This meant growing more vegetables for the family, keeping hens and pigs, as well as fortifying the cellar as a refuge when bombing began, as I felt sure it soon would. There was some satisfaction in taking such precautions but nothing removed the fear of invasion. There was still no demand for plants and from the autumn until the end of 1940 there was every reason to clear much more land for food crops. In any case, the plants left in the ground were now of two year's growth and too large for sale even if there had been a demand. One had, therefore, to be ruthless, and just as the official order came to reduce ornamental nursery stock to one-sixth of the 1939 area, so a nucleus of a few plants of each kind was crammed in with no great hope they would ever be used again even if they survived the war period.

Rather oddly, however, there came a surprising demand for cut flowers. Some had been sent to Birmingham wholesale market in 1940 to bring in a little much needed money as wages for the reduced staff. But by 1941 the Birmingham salesmen who had sold on commission in former market growing days were now clamouring for flowers and returning very good prices. What we sent included several kinds outside the usual range, which previously had no cut flower value. So long as they arrived in saleable condition they filled, it seemed, a need to brighten up the homes of the workers in industry under wartime pressures and scarcity.

At Burwell I had plunged into land reclamation with 300 extra acres of completely derelict land to clear for food production, bringing my commitment down there in the Black Fens to well over 500 acres. It was this commitment, coupled with domestic problems and the loss of confidence in Oakington as a permanent base, which led me to move to Fordham late in 1941. This was a mere three miles from Burwell and the offer of a house coincided with my parents wishing to retire, leaving my brother George to carry on with the nursery at Mildenhall. The relief to be away from roaring bombers at Oakington, with raid warnings and sleepless nights was almost overwhelming. And my three little children were safer and happier in my mother's care, aided by Doris Smith who still supplied their daily needs. At Fordham, Brook House had a little river running through its two acres of ground. Being damned up for a water mill not far down stream, half the land was moist with high trees around and there Father and I dug out the weeds to make beds for primulas, trollius and astilbes and other plants now languishing at Oakington.

With only a hard working skeleton staff the Oakington nursery was cut back by 1943 to only two or three acres of plants. The extra land had been hired and now was back to straight farming. But the vegetables, flowers and some renewal of plant sales by 1943 resulted in a greater net profit than did the 540 acres at Burwell. There, much of the erstwhile derelict land was still under smother crops to kill off the former reed beds, and now that it was better drained, wind erosion was a disability on such light, peaty soil. As the end of the war came closer, so the need to conserve stock nuclei became more urgent and with no intention of ever going back to Oakington I took on a seven-acre field at Fordham for this purpose, working on it during light evenings and at weekends. Father, still spry though well into his seventies, kept the garden at Brook House in good trim, often with my three children, Bridget, Robert and Adrian, for company and dubious help.

It was when I learned that the reclaimed Burwell land adjoining my own was to be allowed to revert by its National Trust owners that I decided to look out for a farm within which the nursery could be restored. But ambivalent feelings assaulted me. Straight farming was so much simpler, much less exacting than a nursery, and though it made sense to combine a restored nursery with farming, my reluctance to plunge into being a full-time plant producer as before was real and persistent. I had kept some contact with the Nursery Trade Association, which now included attendance at meetings of the National Farmers Union, and there was no doubt that the demand for plants would increase. Many of my pre-war customers were by 1945 already wanting to place orders. But so many kinds of plants had perished during the war that it would take an all-out effort to build up stocks again.

Hall Farm, Bressingham, appeared to be just the place to begin again when I signed the contract to purchase it early in 1946, with possession in October of that year. But I was not to know that it would be an exceptionally wet autumn followed by the most severe winter of the century; which in turn was a prelude to a cold spring and a long summer drought. Such weather vagaries were killers, not only of plants, including thousands bought for stock-renewal from Holland, but of the bright hopes I had nurtured of a more settled future. Within a year I had become more unsettled than ever before, until the decision was made to get out and emigrate to Canada. As recounted elsewhere, that decision led, after two years hard labour and much financial loss, to my coming back to a much tougher task at Bressingham than I would have faced had I stayed on. But maybe I needed to endure such a chastening experience to make me realise escapism cannot pay and where my priorities lay.

The first upsets overcome – being dispersed as a family as my house was tenanted – and the offending management booted out, there followed a thankful, purposeful peace of mind. The nursery was in a mess being weedy and badly short of saleable stock. The bank imposed a tight limit on what I could borrow, but frugality was not only tolerable but formed part of the new challenge. The remaining staff showed in the way they worked that they were glad to have me back at the helm. It was tough going working fifteen hours a day, seven days a week, but so rewarding to handle plants again, to propagate, plant and pot, to work with the men hoeing and the women weeding. And to open the mail in which were orders for plants for me to lift and pack for despatch.

To become wholly involved in a project, whatever the motivation, can be so absorbing that others close to one may see it as containing an element of selfishness. Those closest to me were my three children, and although they never accused me of being selfish, their eyes gave away their feelings when I said I was too busy to play or do other things with them. I was still their only parent, and often as I went back to work I had twinges of regret or conscience. My housekeeper with a child of her own helped out, but at least there was ample scope at Bressingham for them all to make their own amusements. Not that I was by any means a remote father figure, nor did I often ask them to do jobs for me. When a rush order came, needing additional help, they showed anything but enthusiasm, and from this I reckoned it would be unlikely that they would ever wish to take over from me. Nor would I ever press them into doing so.

Adding to such thoughts were those which saw some folly in making the principal aim in life going all-out for profit and making the nursery ever larger and more comprehensive. It was one thing to be dedicated to restore the business, but once it was back to its 1939 status then it would be ambition enough to maintain it with full efficiency at that level. But, as I realised within a year of returning from Canada, with closer contacts with the trade, trends were moving away from pre-war attitudes towards gardening. Much emphasis was, for example, being placed on trouble-free ways of gardening. There were articles in the press and talks on the radio about the ways and means by which labour could be reduced now that labour costs had more than doubled. And among the changes recommended to save labour was to switch over to the use of shrubs instead of herbaceous borders and to use ground-cover plants to replace the even more troublesome rockeries and rock gardens.

But such forebodings did not prevent orders for perennials and alpines from increasing as stock increased at Bressingham in the early 1950s. I guessed the reason was that retail nurserymen were finding perennials less profitable to grow and sell, with shrubs and ground-cover plants more in demand. So to meet what demand there was for perennials and alpines it was more economic for these nurserymen to buy in plants for resale. This trend in itself brought a challenge, to keep abreast of the demand by ensuring both quality and good service. The latter called for the prompt despatch of orders, and, with a fairly good memory for the stock position of each kind of plant, I marked each order as it came in to go out at once, if need be, to the packing shed for lifting. In the case of alpines I did the lifting, too – a matter of standing out the items, all pot grown, to be collected and brought to the packing shed. There, Kathy Poulter, who was one of the first to work for me at Bressingham, would transfer the plants from pots to paper wraps for me to pack later on.

Ever since early days at Oakington orders were despatched by rail, except when customers collected their own. It was, until nationalisation, a good service, but even in the 1950s we could be sure of reasonably prompt deliveries to anywhere in the United Kingdom. We had to make sure that packages were secure and this meant a supply of wooden boxes in various sizes. These were bought second-hand from canning factories or egg depots, fish and orange boxes also being used, and great stacks of them were accumulated in advance of each autumn and spring lifting season. When packed and wire strapped they were taken to Diss Station to go mainly by passenger train, for the pre-war promptness by goods train was no longer available. Special rates were obtained by hard bargaining with British Railways, but slowly rail service gave way to road, hastened in the 1960s by the Beeching cuts.

The man in charge who had to lid, strap and take the packed boxes to the station was Don Hubbard, also one of the first Bressingham helpers. His watchword was security and the amount of nails and steel strapping he used went with his oft-repeated remark, 'I'll make sure the railway people don't bust my boxes open.'

To maintain and enhance our standing as wholesale producers also involved growing a wide selection of both standard varieties and new introductions. During the 1950s there was a spate of new Russell lupins, also Michaelmas daisies, irises, delphiniums and phlox. Of each of these twenty to eighty varieties were grown and catalogued, and year by year the list became more comprehensive. In addition there were the choice, rare or incoming new varieties and species which demanded special attention. And sometimes I would take my gamble by making a special launch of some new plant to be first in the field.

All this was exciting, up to a point. But at the back of my mind was the fear that the more the business expanded the more vulnerable we would become should known or unknown factors and hazards hit us. Strikes, storms, floods, frosts, war hostilities and economic slumps were all hovering menaces. I had been caught out in 1939 and by the mid 1950s had become convinced that expansion for its own sake, or merely for profit, should not be a prime objective for me, especially as neither Robert nor Adrian showed any inclination as teenagers to become nurserymen. By 1955 both the acreage under plants and the total stock were twice that of 1939 and there were twice the number of helpers. Having reached that position and continuing my propagandist writings to the gardening press with scores of articles on the value of perennials, I felt a need to deviate.

The first deviation of any consequence was the making in 1955 of the little lake in the nursery by extending a horse pond. The excuse was to use it as an irrigation reservoir, but the real reason was a liking for water and the plants it encouraged – as well to use it for fishing and skating. This project was never to pay off in monetary terms, as I well knew it would not. But whereas some other business projects failed to be profitable for some reason or other beyond my control or from misjudgement, I can look back over 30 years to regard that two-acre lake as a very good investment indeed in terms of its mature beauty and the pleasure it has given, one way and another, to me and to others.

Making the new island beds in front of my house was not a deviation. But it added a new dimension to the existing garden and, after a while, set me on my way to making a new garden. In between nursery duties from 1957 to 1962 about an acre a year of additional garden was carved out in the adjoining meadow. Almost all the pastures were island beds carved out to fit in with slopes and mature trees. This served many nursery requirements – for trials, stocks and a supply of seeds, and, to some extent, to provide a shop window for the plants. What creativeness I possessed was given full vent, but there were two vital factors to spur me on. One was my love of plants and a yearning to see as wide a variety being grown as possible. The other was to prove the value of perennials grown as naturally as possible in order to counter the criticism of them being labour intensive. That now, thirty years later, perennials are more in demand than ever before, is some vindication and a source of enormous gratification to me.

Back in 1956 there were still some enthusiasts in addition to me who believed that perennials were not deserving of neglect. It occurred to me that if they could be attracted to a fostering society it would help, and a few telephone calls and letters led to the formation and my chairmanship of the Hardy Plant Society. Although for several years it did some good work, it did not expand to any great extent until quite recent times. Now it is flourishing with area branches in England, and some have been formed in America with affiliation to the parent body. And, on its 21st anniversary, I was honoured with the title of President, even though I did very little for it after the first few years.

Garden-making had to be a more or less spare time job. But during the later 1950s I left more of the detailed work of the nursery to others willing to take responsibility. Apart from Mary Fox who so competently ran the office, there was Bob Hill who, avid for more responsibility, supervised field work to an increasing extent. Then, in 1962, it became clear that both Robert and Adrian would after all come home. Robert had left home to learn farming, and Adrian, having wandered off to America, found his interest in plants was growing steadily. But their presence was seen by Bob Hill as a threat to his position, despite my assurances that there was plenty of scope for him as well, and a year or two later he left. Robert at first preferred farming, but had a flair for things mechanical and largely through him the nursery gradually became mechanised. Adrian, however, having settled down after working to gain experience in Swiss and Danish nurseries, had other ideas than to follow, as he said one day, in my footsteps. He wanted to work up his own special preference for conifers and heathers. Nor could I blame him, reflecting how adamant I had been in telling my father I wanted to follow my own bent. But in giving a qualified blessing to Adrian I thought it necessary to advise him against growing too many kinds. About twenty kinds each of conifer and heathers, I suggested, would be about right in view of our wholesale status and to avoid complications on the production level.

Adrian's lack of comment on this advice was taken as concurrence, but before long I had given approval for a new propagating greenhouse specifically for conifers and heathers. There were some teething troubles with batches of cuttings dying off, but once over these stocks increased. And so did the range of both types of plant.

When he married Rosemary in 1966 the site they selected for their home was in a six-acre meadow, secluded at the end of a narrow cul de sac lane. Almost at once Adrian began planting conifers and heathers as a garden, ostensibly for stock but also to experiment with ways of growing them in association in island beds. Having begun he then, I suppose, took his cue from the way my garden had expanded a few years earlier. In acquiring more and more conifers, mainly dwarf kinds, it became a trial ground not only for these in variety but for their association with other plants, trees, shrubs and perennials. Now, the whole field is taken over and the range of conifers is in the region of a thousand species, forms and cultivars. And of these, about ten times the number I suggested should be the limit for those produced for sale, are listed in the catalogue and occupying about forty acres of the nursery.

This is part of the story of how the business expanded once Robert and Adrian gained control. It was not a case of them forcing my hand. I kenw the time would have to come for me to hand over, and when, at the usual retiring age, I decided to give up the practice of opening and checking the mail, then my time was up as supremo. Since at the time I was up to my neck in another deviation, setting up a steam engine museum, I had only minor qualms. Both sons had proved their ability and their commitment to what I considered to be sound business principles. On business policy there were some grounds for dissention. I could only advise them to expand slowly, to avoid becoming vulnerable and overstretched financially. Against their belief that a business must expand or go back, my arguments in favour of consolidation did not cut much ice. And although my misgivings have continued, I cannot but admire what they have achieved in making what I began so haltingly sixty years ago: one of the foremost nurseries in Britain.

Until 1965 I was still firmly of the opinion that the nursery should grow only for the trade, but it was having my garden open to the public on specified days which prised open the door to selling plants directly to the public as well. Visitors saw plants in my garden which were not to be seen in garden centres – or in many other gardens or retailers catalogues for that matter. To their enquiries the stock answer was that they should obtain them from their retailer, who in turn would order from us. But this did not work. Most retailers were more than reluctant to take the trouble to supply them, and, feeling sympathy for those who wished to acquire these uncommon plants, we decided to cater for them in some way. My chief anxiety was a wish not to take business away from the retailers we supplied, and this has been a long-standing policy.

Our first retail catalogue offered only a limited range of plants, confined to, as we thought, the less common subjects, mainly perennials since there were already several specialists offering a wide range of alpines. A catalogue by itself, however, was not enough, and in that year – after a lapse of thirty years – we staged an exhibit at Chelsea Flower Show. The result was quite remarkable. There was a keen interest in the range of plants staged in an island bed setting and a goodly number of orders were booked, including some from other nurserymen. For years we had grown and offered the rather unusual *Rheum alexandrae* – a rhubarb species with quite spectacular yellow-lipped flower bracts. Of the two hundred or so we had been growing for several years, yearly sales averaged no more than twenty, in spite of it being low priced for a rarity. But at that Chelsea Show a hundred and fifty were booked, about half wholesale and half retail. Ironically, the stock became depleted as a result and over-intensive efforts to propagate led to losses so that for the past ten years it has become too scarce to offer any more for sale.

The past ten years has seen, contrary to expectations, wholesale orders increasing as the retail side of the business expanded. Chelsea exhibits have become larger and more comprehensive and the retail catalogue likewise, especially since it has been illustrated in colour.

CHAPTER FOUR

Plants and People

It touches my vanity, my conceit, or self-esteem to be referred to as a plantsman. To me this is the greatest of compliments, but I squirm inwardly to be called an expert, just as I react strongly at any suggestion of being an authority on plants or a tycoon in business. All these infer pre-eminence, of having achieved a status where little or nothing more has to be learned. Such a position is out of reach of anyone, however clever or knowledgeable they may be. For in the world of plants no one can possibly know more than some of the answers, either in terms of successful cultivation or being familiar with the immense range of plants available. Some specialists in, say, roses, rhododendrons or daffodils might be worthy of the 'expert' title, but not otherwise. Plantsman is a less pretentious term. It embraces those who are devoted to plants of almost any kind; whose love for them over the years, as practical cultivators, has brought knowledge and experience. And almost always this engenders a kind of humility, with the awareness that one will never know or grow more than a portion of what exists somewhere or other.

A true plantsman is as aware of his failures as of his successes and is never fully content or satisfied, aiming for perfection, which he knows will never be attained. Here a fault in the language crops up, because it sounds clumsy to attach the term plantswoman to those of the opposite sex, especially as there are probably more women than men worthy of holding the title. As my thoughts range over my gardening friends and acquaintances, women outnumber men. But, as I have mentioned elsewhere, plants and gardening are unique in attracting both sexes on an equal footing, eliminating the largely artificial and harmful aspects of the socially conditioned polarity between the sexes. In view of this, should we settle then, in the modern idiom, on plantsperson as the most appropriate designation?

It is surely a vital part of the plantsperson's life to be close to nature, to be aware of the contributing or governing factors, such as the soil, the weather, heat and cold and that the soil itself is alive with bacteria and worms that do good, and other 'creepy crawlies' that do harm. I must revert to the first person plural hoping that I am worthy of the title of plantsman and say that we have few illusions about our own place in nature. It is a privilege, whether or not we deserve it, to feel in tune with nature, at least when natural forces do not thwart our efforts; and even then relations are restored and a new balance is reached. It is then that the joys make us forget past disappointments and frustrations. We dig, ready for planting, adding an unspoken blessing to the extra goodness we put into the soil – the compost we make or the fertiliser or peat we buy. Turning over the soil we are on the lookout for pernicious weeds to pick up, and doing our best to avoid hurting worms. Some of us may whisper an apology to an accidentally severed worm, with the hope that it will be able to grow a new rear end. Some of us have a robin or blackbird hovering around hopefully, and then a quirkish decision has to be made – whether to toss a worm to the bird, watching how greedily and cleverly it is swallowed, or be single-minded and allow the worm to return to its element where it benefits soil fertility.

Unalloyed pleasure comes to both bird and digger if a grub or slug is found to be flicked to where beady eyes can see it. Robins are as voracious as blackbirds and thrushes, and although it is surprising how much their crops will hold, they approach large worms with caution. If a few smart pecks fail to reduce its length, they will usually leave it alone, severely mauled but not mortally wounded. But the larger birds prefer to take large worms away and devour them at leisure – or at nesting time collect a beakful, one after the other, without dropping any before flying off to feed their young. There appear to me to be far more male than female blackbirds in my garden, and I suspect that some are bachelors, judging by the relative few that sing. Bird song is said to be an assertion of territorial rights, in which case unmated males would have nothing to declare.

The twenty or so other species of birds which nest in my garden are more secretive, except in wintry weather when they flock to the food on the bird table outside the kitchen window. In early summer they are heard but not seen because then one's gaze is directed at things growing nearer the ground. When young I was not too busy to snoop around seeking out their nests, just out of interest and admiration for their nesting habits, and the delicate beauty of their eggs. Top marks always go to the long-tailed tits with a domed nest which no human could ever copy exactly; so different to the doves and pigeons which lazily place together a few twigs in which to lay a couple of eggs against the ten or twelve of the long-tailed tit.

There was also a time when I used to leave a row of strawberries unnetted for the birds to eat, as an act of appreciation for the pleasure their singing gave me. But when they showed after a few years that they still persisted in finding ways into the netting, and, after a feast, forgot where the entry hole was located, I gave up the practice and put up with having to make a way for them to fly out rather than chase and catch them for release.

Such asides in a gardener's life are all part of being close to nature, but our closest attention is centred on our plants, such as the special care we give to those new to us. Always make the planting hole deep and wide enough to avoid crushing or crumpling the roots. Press the plant in lightly if the soil is wet or sticky, especially in autumn or winter, for frost will penetrate more deeply into compacted soil, which if it is not planted deeply enough it may lift to expose its roots to drying March winds.

We know better than to insert plants when the soil is dry, and give a sprinkling of water over the surface. Spring planting has its special risks and firming is important. But in dry soil which tends to trickle back into the hole a surface-sprinkle is not good enough. What we do in such conditions is to partially fill the hole with soil after the plant is inserted and then fill it to the brim with water. Then, when this has soaked away, we draw in the rest of the soil, and, by firming it with fingers rather than the foot, leave an inch of loose, dry tilth which will not go crusty. The crusty surface which follows overhead watering as the soil dries off prevents its aeration and the capillary action so vital to plant growth.

Probably the most frequent question put by people who buy plants, especially of potted, indoor plants, is 'How often does it need watering?' To this there is only one answer and to those who are not plantspeople it seldom satisfies. The right answer is, of course, only when it needs it, for, although different kinds of plants have differing water requirements, few people seem able to judge either by feel or sight when soil is wet or dry, whereas a plantsperson can tell at a glance or by a finger-tip feel. Most plants indicate thirst by drooping, but more are killed by over-watering which often does not show up on the leaves or flowers until they begin to drop off – and then it is mostly too late to be remedied.

Generally speaking, it is much better for plants, whether in pots or in the open ground, to draw what moisture they require upwards rather than from above. Some reference is made to this in Chapter Two, 'Wet and Dry', but a little more stress needs to be placed on the harmful effects of inadequate overhead watering. A good gardener does not have to be told that one good soaking is better than several frequent splashes which do not penetrate more than an inch or two, to leave the feeding or drinking roots of some plants still dry. Or that to keep the surface inch or so of soil loose helps moisture retention. There was a time when I went to considerable trouble to carry out my belief that sub-irrigation was superior. Trenches were dug 3ft apart and about 18in deep in which a grid of 4in land-drain pipes were laid. A slight fall was given so that as water from a hose entered from the raised end it would fill the whole system and soak outwards into the soil to be available to the plants' roots. It worked well to begin with, but then the pipes became silted up or one or two became dislodged, and, as the garden area expanded, it became troublesome to segregate these two beds when forty others had to come under overhead soakings.

Had I prepared a master plan before embarking on this five-acre extension, carried out bit by bit over a period of five years, it would have saved an enormous amount of time to lay a proper, permanent irrigation system instead of dragging hoses and suchlike from bed to bed, from which spray standards are stuck in the ground to give full coverage. In a drought the whole garden has to be watered weekly by this means, which takes two helpers about twenty man hours to perform. For a peat bed made more recently a better system operates.

The bed is on the north side of a high wall and a small-bore plastic water pipe is fixed near its top, having mist spray nozzles at intervals, so that by turning on a tap the whole bed of about 70ft by 8 to 9ft can be moistened. This bed, by the way, is not entirely of peat, but a mixture of 20 per cent soil, 20 per cent bark, 10 per cent sharp sand and 50 per cent peat, and the plants have taken to it very well.

Although moisture control is of vital importance, one does not need to be obsessed by it. Nor are any of the plantspersons I know fussy or pernickety in their gardening habits. They may have certain basic rules on cultivation and after care which they stick to as a result of experience, but they seldom indulge in chores and practices they consider unnecessary. They may neglect such niceties as the dead-heading of fading flowers for the sake of appearances, and may even see beauty in them. The well-being of the plants themselves is more important than such niceties as spickness, and weeds are, to them, much more of a menace to good gardening. They are much too alert and aware of jobs they want to do to bother with those which have no real bearing on the well-being of their treasures. Such people, too, are usually well integrated as individuals and are philosophical about their own limitations.

Not every good gardener comes into the green-fingered category. One sometime hears boastful remarks from those who believe it is their special gift, but their prowess does not always stand up to close investigation. A true gardener is not, as a rule, a boastful person and will usually admit to failures more readily than to successes, which they may dismiss as luck rather than expertise. Being green-fingered is not so much a mysterious knack of making seeds come up, cuttings root and plants in general flourish which, for ordinary mortals, would fail. If it is a gift at all I fancy it is due to having a caring nature, of being able to see things from the plant's point of view – coupled with a deftness of touch and maybe a dash of faith rather than hope. Some people talk to their plants, and perhaps there is a kind of ESP at work which defies rational explanation.

Claire was not such a person, although she had a genuine love of plants. She came to us as a learner assistant with a university degree. After finding no satisfaction in other kinds of work she became convinced that horticulture was what she really wanted to practise as a career. Like any other novice she took her turn with such jobs as weeding, but soon was given more intimate tasks such as pricking off or lining out seedlings and propagating from cuttings. I put up with her slowness as long as I could, hoping she would speed up with greater confidence and familiarity with the plants. But, when the time came to tell her the pace had to quicken, she confessed that she had already tried to do so. Her fingers, she said, were all thumbs when handling small delicate plants, and not even the demonstrations I had given her made any difference. There was nothing for her but to leave and try some other profession. One could not help feeling sorry for her, even though on six months' performance she had never earned her pay.

I am not suggesting that plantspersons are superior to anyone else in terms of human virtue. My knowledge of them and my appraisal has been almost entirely confined to the common interests we share in plants. Their private lives have been largely beyond my ken, just as mine has been beyond theirs. Our conversations are almost always centred on the inexhaustible subject of plants, which tends to rule out revelations of more personal a nature. In a vague sense gardening at this level is a kind of club with no organisation and no rules, except that we shy away from those who are mean where swaps or sharing are concerned, or pedantic when nomenclature is discussed. Such people are, by common consent, apt to be unacceptable for full membership.

This reminds me of F.L. As a late comer, developing a garden after retirement, he was in something of a hurry to build up a collection of plants with a view to bringing in some monetary return. Some of his stock he bought from me, and once, on saying he wished to collect to save on carriage, he asked to be put up for the night rather than stay at a hotel before returning to Devon. Flora, my wife, willingly agreed. But instead of going home next morning he decided to visit some other East Anglian gardens and asked if he could stay a second night, or possibly two more. Not wishing to be inhospitable to a quite elderly gentleman, we agreed but with some misgivings which proved to be only too well founded. Each evening he returned in good time for dinner and for two or three hours dominated the conversation with boring anecdotes and accounts of his successes and complaints. I longed to see the back of him and wished I had not gone round the garden with him in the first place, giving him bits and pieces of plants he fancied. We had called in at his place a year or so before and he had offered nothing, with the explanation that, as yet, he had nothing to spare which would interest me.

F.L. was the opposite, for instance, to such as the late Margery Fish who even tried to persuade me to accept, on a few occasions, one of only two or three plants she possessed by putting a spade through a single clump. Or the very generous Maurice Mason whose usual response to a request was either to help ourselves or make notes which would result in great bundles of plants being sent. One's heart naturally warms to such people, to the extent that I feel uneasy if what they ask for in return represents less than equal reciprocity. It is a fairly common practice among gardening friends to take along a few plants when visiting them after a lapse of a year or two. One has to select subjects, if possible, which they may not have already, and this is not often at all easy. But it is as much a pleasure to the giver as to the receiver to find that one has succeeded in this aim. And one can be pretty sure that the friend will find something different for you to take home.

Swopping has been mentioned before, and it is a delightful means of acquiring plants to add to one's collections. Giving on impulse leads to a compulsive urge to collect even though, for a professional nursery-man, somewhat against business principles. In terms of sharing, it is all to the good, and many a plant I have acquired by this means has become available to the gardening public, because I find the urge to propagate a rare garden worthy plant irresistible, as well as rewarding if it creates a demand for what might otherwise remain in obscurity and something of a Cinderella.

With less stamina nowadays for heavy work, propagating takes up more of my time and interest. Having a few acres under my charge, apart from the garden, we produce for the nursery about 400 different kinds of plants needing special care. This involves hand digging and planting and the provision of varying soil, shade or moisture requirements for quite large quantities, sometimes, apart from the stock-building process of some special subjects until I consider it is safe to let the nursery take it over. It is, however, not unknown for a stock to be built up and sent to the nursery where, for some reason, it is not happy and so has to come back permanently. In addition to myself, four full time and three part timers look after a total of about four acres where plants are grown in rows as well as the five-acre display garden, which takes up less than half the total labour requirement now that we are as fully organised as it is possible to be.

Seasonal routine is not only unavoidable but is the major reason why the work is so interesting, and the time seems to fly by swiftly. Propagating in one form or another takes place the whole year round. In the dead of winter certain kinds of plants can be safely lifted and divided, and also planted except when it simply is not fit to work outdoors due to rain, frost or snow. A season's work begins in August, for it is then that such subjects as the early-flowering adonis, caltha, primulas, trilliums and so on are dormant but in the process of making new roots. As with other subjects which are in the catalogue, a batch of mature plants is lifted and graded, some for sale and some to be divided and replanted. In many cases a planting has to stay down for two years in order to attain sufficient size and maturity, and this involves planting two batches of each with quantities varying according to present or future demand.

During the autumn three helpers spend much of their time lifting orders, which are sent across to the packing shed to join those being drawn from the main nursery. During those weeks – from late September to early December – some 300 to 350 individual retail orders are executed every day, with wholesale orders almost a separate department. September and October are the months when most cuttings are taken to be inserted in the frames or in boxes under glass. Some of these are in quite small numbers. Either they are of subjects which are not reliably hardy, to provide a reserve to fall back on if losses occur in the garden, or they are of new acquisitions in the process of being increased. The latter are liable to be raided for cuttings whenever there is sufficient growth, and these are under my ministrations as the judge of their future value. In December, up come some quite large batches of plants for dividing under cover. Brunneras, pulmonarias, bergenias and symphytums are followed by hostas, rodgersias, cimicifugas, filipendulas and such like. Space is made for them in a rather old span glasshouse where they are piled up in trays, with, in cold weather, a blower heater being used to take the chill off their damp, cold roots. Even then the fingers are apt to become numbed from their chill, as one teases them apart, grading and counting as they go back into trays for sale or planting.

Some kinds are dealt with in the potting shed where it is more snug in wintry weather. But here there is no room for plants in bulk, and the bench is often used on which to pot a wide variety of less common kinds for later sale at the Plant Centre. Once potted they are placed just outside where adequate after-care can be given. February brings the spring retail order season, weather permitting, and, until the end of March or early April, the planters can only deal with what divisions are ready in between lifting orders. But growth is about to begin on more large batches which are best planted in spring, and, as fast as those already divided go out for planting, astilbes, trollius, polygonums, pyrethrums come on for me to divide and grade in that order, ending always with kniphofias in April or May. Counting as I work becomes such a habit as to be almost automatic, even when it isn't necessary.

As a general rule, I find that plants which flower before mid-June are best divided and replanted in early autumn. Later summer or autumn flowering kinds are best dealt with in spring, and this has become the basis of our seasonal routine. As for propagating from green cuttings, there is no general rule applicable. Some do best from basal growth in spring, others from tips or heel cuttings later on. Much of what I have learned has been through trial and error – and I am still learning. And although some cuttings will root more evenly and quickly under mist and above bottom heat, some very heavy losses have occurred on the nursery when this method has been used, to offset a usually high success rate among the millions of cuttings treated there under modern controlled conditions. The high humidity of mist propagation is resented by most plants native to a dryish climate – an origin often coinciding with the possession of grey foliage.

Root cuttings as a rule are best taken from plants which, though still dormant, are about to renew spring growth. Plants such as phlox and *Anemone japonica* can be safely dealt with in December, as cut up, scattered sections, but the latter need to be protected from frost penetration. Root cuttings from those plants which shoot from sections of fleshy root – anchusas, eryngiums, papavers, verbascums, etc. – are all safe to take before new growth begins. But when dealing with such choice alpines as some of the geraniums, morisia and *Crepis incana*, extra care is needed. One of my mean streaks is to be chary of giving away any secrets regarding the propagation of tricky subjects which I have learned the hard way. Maybe it is selfish and maybe not. The raiser of *Thalictrum delavayi* Hewitt's Double kept his propagating secret close to his chest and it took me years of trial and error to crack it. If anyone is able to do the same with a few difficult plants which I have mastered, good luck to them, but I still see no good reason for broadcasting special techniques I have learned.

CHAPTER FIVE

Faith, Hope and Charity

Faith has a rather different connotation for gardeners than for the religious minded. In the religious sense faith is, or is said to be, concerned with the substance of things unknown. It is a belief in what cannot be seen or proven in a tangible way, a kind of prop or defence against the visible odds being realities. But, according to the Bible, faith is an attribute powerful enough to move mountains and to work miracles of healing. To succeed in some superhuman effort or performance one needs to have faith in one's ability as well as having divine inspiration; but, for gardeners, faith is usually a matter of believing entirely in one's self. If we know how to set about some creative act of gardening and what is required to see it through, all will be well so long as we are not thwarted by adverse weather, pests, diseases, accidents and the like. These we may have been aware of as risks and hazards. Hope in such circumstances is far more relevant and sensible than faith. Experience gives us faith that natural seasonal rhythms will not go haywire and lead to failures.

For gardeners, hope is an essential ingredient. It is quite inconceivable that anyone could even begin gardening without hope as the spur, and I fancy that this applies to any creative undertaking no matter what the motivation. Because there are so many variable factors which affect gardening, we can seldom be sure enough to have faith in success. But hope springs eternal and if failure comes through adverse weather or other cause beyond one's control, it is hope that prompts us to try again. Not always, however, by the same means or under the same conditions, because if we're willing to ponder over a loss, we may find a surge of renewed hope come to us, having seen the reason for a failure. Or we may just, by trial and error, find the right place for a plant which displayed an aversion to the spot first selected for it. Hope and perseverance therefore go hand in hand, and, by employing the latter, encouraged by the former, we are storing up knowledge. Knowledge gained by practical experience is the kind we are never likely to forget, for it is well-rooted in human nature not to repeat costly mistakes.

When first I procured that little blue charmer *Corydalis cashmeriana* I knew very little of its requirements but only that it was tricky, especially away from the high humidity of its native habitat. Lacking a cool spot not starved by tree roots, I planted it on a north-sloping bank above a pool, and though it flowered it did not flourish. After two years it had made almost no increase but hopes rose after I moved it where there was more moisture, with peat added to the loam. But it fared no better there, nor did it when transferred to a spot with more shade. The fourth move was to a semi-shaded ledge next to another sulky beauty, *Thalictrum diffusiforme*, for which leaf mould and sharp sand had been used with some, though not much, success. Here the corydalis began to expand. Visiting plantsmen had said East Anglia was no place for such a plant, and, apart from hearing commendations, it was a joy to see that marvellous display of blue in late spring. Not that it flourished as I had seen it at Keillour Castle in Perthshire, but well enough to try some in pots. To my surprise it grew even better and after several years the stock increased sufficiently to part with some each year. Now, in a north-facing peat bed, it grows well enough to lift and divide every year after flowering.

For every success such as this, a label could be found among a box full in the tool shed of some choice subject which has refused to grow, perhaps after repeated trial. One has to be philosophical and realistic. It is easy to blame the plant for being fussy, miffy or unadaptable, but it should not, in fairness, be condemned on that account. Every kind of plant has its own limits of adaptability, and if we fail to provide conditions within that limitation it is our fault and not that of the plant. There are, of course, some plants which cannot tolerate a given climate, quite apart from considerations of soil, shade or moisture, and perhaps the greatest bugbear of our English climate is the dampness of winter, the lack of reliable snow cover, the rapid changes from frost to rain which occur so often from November to March. It is asking too much of plants native to high altitudes and to predictably regular seasonal changes of rainfall and temperature, humidity and dryness, to expect that all of these which we attempt to grow outdoors will succeed in England. But we keep on trying, and one or two outstanding successes will come as a stimulation to jaded hopes.

For me, at least, winter is the season when hope is in the ascendant. As colour in the garden fades with autumn the memory of failings, and maybe losses, are still fresh, and thoughts occur now and then on causes and remedies. Not that I expect to ever attain perfection. That state has eluded me for so long as to become a will o'the wisp, beckoning always but forever out of reach. From experience, too, comes the underlying fear that notes I make during summer of improvements to put into effect later may not all be carried out. It happens every year – this group to be divided and replanted, that one to be moved because it fails to blend or keep good company with its neighbours and so on. But when planting time ends and anticipated jobs have not all been carried out, others not so listed have been fitted in, mostly on impulse.

Hope is strongest in the dead of winter for that is not the time one should be active among the beds of plants. If it is not too wet it is too cold, and work is confined to digging, pruning, or, in my case, propagating dormant roots. Such repetitive work under cover is conducive to a wide range of meditations and resolutions. Such and such a plant failed or fell short of perfection because of this and that, or the weather was to blame. But next season will be better with clement weather to bless whatever course of action I decide to take, never forgetting or overlooking the need to work with nature. Except, of course, when the opportunity comes to thwart her, to my own or the plant's advantage.

It is my good fortune to nurse another dimension for hope. Every year, mostly as a result of swops, there are fresh subjects to add to my collection. Some I may not have seen growing or in flower and there is always hopeful anticipation that they may prove to be special, or sufficiently garden worthy to set about propagating them by one means or another to be evaluated or discovered. Or they may come as seeds collected in the wild from far off places, as a result of contributing to the cost of some plant-hunting expedition. Not that one should bank on their germination, but if they do come up and are reared to flowering stage they will be exciting additions.

The most excitement comes when a batch of seedlings comes into flower, having been raised in hope of a new break or improvements in existing varieties. Not that I have personally taken the trouble to do much hybridising. For many years this was undertaken by Percy Piper, who had been gardener-handyman to the previous owner of Bressingham Hall Farm. Percy was one of those nature-loving countrymen with a devotion and loyalty to which one had to respond by giving him insights and outlets for the skills he longed to develop. He sought encouragement more than praise and monetary reward, and he set about 'fiddling', as he called the rudimentary hybridising techniques I explained to him, with emasculating scissors and a camel hair brush for the transfer of pollen on the subjects I suggested he should work on. Over the years he raised many batches of seedlings – erigerons, heucheras, crocosmias, kniphofias, pyrethrums and several others. As they came into flower he and I assessed their qualities, staking any that stood out and whittling down the selection year after year until the very best were given names under which stocks could be worked up and offered eventually for sale.

Percy's 'fiddling' began in 1947 with heucheras. To find a batch of over 2,000 which he had planted about to flower in 1950, soon after my return from the disastrous Canadian venture, was a benison I scarcely deserved. The hours spent surveying the beauty, the entrancing variety in form and colour as the first selections were made, had a tonic effect on me – just what was needed as I was about to take up again what I should never have left. More about heucheras follows, but from that batch were selected and named eight which some years later went into the Wisley Trials and all were either Highly Commended or given Awards of Merit, whilst one, 'Scintillation', gained a First Class Certificate. In his quiet, unobtrusive way Percy included in his 'fiddling' some subjects outside the recommendations I suggested to him. He had not been prompted to fiddle with dwarf hardy geraniums, but it appeared to him to use *G. subcaulescens* to put more colour into *G. cinereum*. The result was 'Ballerina' and it proved to be such a good plant as to be included in almost every alpine plant catalogue both in Europe and America.

But as with a coin, so hope has two sides. It may well spring eternal, but hope deferred sickens the heart. So it was with the new breaks in pyrethrums under Percy's fiddling. I 'went a bundle' on a new one named 'Abendglut' – probably raised in Germany, but the main stock appeared in Denmark and its unusual salmon colour prompted me to go there to secure distribution rights for Britain in 1953. It grew well enough and sold quite well, but it had weak stems. Percy set about crossing it with others we had and from the resultant seedlings some years later, six were selected. Two were improvements on the variety now anglicised as 'Evenglow', one of them being even richer in colour. Others included singles and some doubles from the shell-pink of 'Venus' to such a deep shade as to merit the name 'Inferno'. In a matter of five years, by simple division in spring, there were enough to be included in our wholesale catalogue. But in that year growth had been tardy and flowering sparse and stunted. A virus was diagnosed by plant pathologists with the usual recommendation to burn all infected plants.

But nurserymen and gardeners do not share the same kind of mentality as plant pathologists, and to burn all infected plants would have been to destroy ten years work along with all our hopes centred on some outstanding new cultivars. We tried lime and soot and fresh soil for them, but stocks slowly dwindled. It was as if they had a kind of sleepy sickness, some varieties languishing more than others. When 'Venus' was reduced to three miserable pieces, with 'Vanessa' the strongest at fifty pieces, strangely the weakly 'Evenglow' was surviving better than any of the new ones, whilst 'Inferno', which had begun strongly, had died out. It was sad to see, and experiments were put in hand using sharp sand, lime and lots of old farm muck, along with dustings of Captan. Where all these additives were used liberally, plants began to perk up and so the slow, tedious process of building up stocks began again on the four survivors – 'Ariel', 'Taurus', 'Vanessa' and 'Apollo', together with a few other, older varieties. It is still proceeding, but now that outdoor commercial flower growing is in eclipse, the demand comes only from the gardening public, whereas at one time I grew about 100,000 pyrethrum plants in forty different varieties.

Times have radically changed in market growing as well as nursery production and outlets. When wages were ninepence an hour for seasonal workers in the industry, and when fruit and flowers went to distant markets by rail, there was no lack of people wanting to cut flowers and pick fruit. But now that the rate of pay is £2 an hour few are attracted. And even if road delivery to markets is simpler than by rail, market returns do not reflect the same rate of inflation as do wages.

There are no grounds for hope that outdoor flower growing will ever come back as a thriving industry. There are, however, grounds for both faith and hope that the love of gardening will become more widespread, if only because it is the perfect antidote to the pressures of modern life. But what about charity? At first there appears to be no connection, no link horticulturally between these three, unless we replace charity with love as being of the same root. Paul the Apostle was doubtless thinking of charity as the kind of love which embraces both the Divine and the neighbourly. Under the accepted meaning of charity there are a large number of people who open their gardens and who devote the proceeds to charitable causes. It costs the owners of such gardens very little to do this, and, whether or not pride comes into the reckoning, it ranks as a commendable practice and many a good cause would miss out if the practice were for some reason ruled out of order. According to the tax laws, it is, as I learned to my cost. Due to the war and subsequent moves, it was not until the late 1950s that Sunday openings for charitable causes resumed. At Oakington in the late 1930s there was the nursery to see and flowers to buy, cut by volunteers. Being wholesale only, this was no departure into selling to the public and there was no thought of tax liability. Nor was there when the new garden at Bressingham provided the opportunity of donations from gate receipts. From a hundred or two pounds for the National Society for the Prevention of Cruelty to Children and the Gardeners' Royal Benevolent Society in 1958 it increased to several thousands annually by 1968. But, in setting up a steam engine museum and applying for its charitable status as a trust, the Inland Revenue demanded a full account of not only monies paid to charities, but personal accounts as well – as a check no doubt on integrity. Being in the clear on this regard was no mitigation for tax liability on the £33,000 paid to good causes from 'gate receipts', and after a long and costly fight with the tax authorities I had to pay £12,500 in back tax – in addition to £6,000 for professional services. In an interview with the tax inspector, he blandly informed me that all receipts from public openings for whatever cause are taxable as income and according to the letter of the law. 'Then why pick on such as me?' was my complaint. Suavely he said, 'Not worth the bother of collecting when it's only a few hundred. Yours was.'

Garden owners beware. It may be your pleasure as it was mine to open to the public and thereby make donations to good causes. But the more you collect, whether from entrance money or what you may sell at a profit, be it produce or refreshments, is regarded by the tax man as additional to your income and therefore liable for tax – if he applies the letter of the law. And the larger the sums you collect and distribute the more likely you are to be selected for clobbering. For several years I was in the habit of giving quite large quantities of plants to local hospital gardens and to old folks homes coming under local authorities. This, too, gave me pleasure even it if was against trade association recommendations. But suspecting that as trading stock it had a book value and was therefore taxable, the practice had to be discontinued.

Establishing the steam museum as a charitable trust ruled out direct donations to other charities. As a trust, designed to carry on beyond my lifetime, no income tax is payable, but no charities are exempt from VAT which knocks off fifteen per cent of gate receipts on open days. The gate and parking arrangements are still manned by volunteers acting on behalf of several charitable institutions, and what we pay for their services is handed over to them, putting them and us in the clear. I mention this because it might suggest a way out for any readers who feel under a threat as a result of my revelation. So long as the extra staff are volunteers and represent a registered charity – such as the National Gardens Scheme – they need have no fear. Extra staff paid wages out of takings are, however, with their employers, strictly on the wrong side of the law, which might come down upon them if a considerable amount of money is involved, and those in doubt would do well to consult an accountant – even if mine gave no warning at the time that I was in breach of the tax law.

Another aspect of charity should be mentioned, although it is on the fringe in an interpretive sense. Some gardeners are by nature generous and it is a pleasure for them to give plants, seeds or cuttings to their friends. Such gifts are not in the best interests of the nursery trade but most nurserymen survive in spite of it being an age-old practice which will never cease. The only aspect of it to be condemned is when a garden owner has a surplus of some rapid-growing, invasive plant – such as Snow in Summer (cerastium) or Gardener's Garters (phalaris). Gifts of such plants confer no blessing and if the recipient is new to gardening or less than knowledgeable, initial thanks are likely to turn to curses in due course.

A conscientious garden owner would, of course, warn an unsuspecting friend in such cases, and those who are both genuine and generous are worthy to be called true gardeners. Which brings in the truer, wide definition of charity – as plant lovers. It could even be said that all true gardeners must be plant lovers. For them, whatever their speciality may be (and if they have one), plants are not just decorative material. They are living things, with their own individual characteristics, responsive to loving care in enticing them to give of their best – often as strangers in a strange land. The most devoted gardeners who go in for variety rather than massed displays of a few kinds of plants just for effect, or for the pride it gives them, regard their plants almost as if they were their children. If they possess a competitive spirit it is usually to have success in growing rare of difficult plants.

Some such devotees may be by nature jealous of others' success where they have failed; or their possessiveness makes them mean, unwilling to give or share even when they have a surplus. One finds these human traits coming out when swopping occurs. It seems to be the rule for some to part with only the smallest possible piece of plant or just an odd cutting or two even if they could well afford to spare enough to give the other party a good start. One cannot help feelings of disgust welling up when, having sent sizeable plants for such an exchange, those subsequently received in return are so tiny that at least a year's nursing is required before they will flower.

It has been said that the surest way of keeping a rare or difficult plant is to give half one's stock away. In principle this has some merit, because, if a loss occurs, there should be another source from which a replacement could be made. In practice, however, it is somewhat fraught with risks – such as loss with both halves failing to survive, perhaps as a result of making the gift. A realistic sharing is a very different matter. If there is enough of a rarity to spare, and if a request comes from a skilled, devoted gardener, then it is by way of a shared insurance as well as a shared pleasure. Trust is called for and so is a certain awareness of what motivates those who make specific requests. I prefer those who say, 'Yes please, if you're sure you can spare it' when responding to my offer to dig up a plant from a group.

Only last year I walked round my garden with someone – a well known amateur gardener – who was on his second visit. Two years before he had requested ten or a dozen different kinds, in return for which he had sent me a few seeds. This time I suspected that he was on the cadge, yet I couldn't bring myself to charge him for them since they were not nursery plants but from my own garden. Months later I was being shown round his own garden and came away disappointed and disillusioned, for only one or two of the plants he had ever had from me were to be seen and no offers made to balance the uneven exchange. Instead, there were references to winter losses and to thieves, but, as excuses, they were not very convincing. I had an inkling that his gardening and his collecting was tainted with profits on the sly, and there will be a negative response to any further requests he may make to visit. Even for gardeners, the pathway of charity and love has many openings, as well as being strewn more with snags and pitfalls than with faith and hope.

CHAPTER SIX

Enamoured Ambitions

Among nurserymen Percy Picton, who died only recently, stood very high indeed for he also was a plantsman. Such a comment implies that some nurserymen are not plantsmen, and this is true when they are businessmen first and foremost. Young Percy was, no doubt, encouraged by William Robinson of Gravetye for whom he worked for a time, but his love of plants probably began before that memorable experience. A few years ago I renewed my acquaintance with Percy at his Colwall nursery, calling in without prior notice. He was at one end of a greenhouse as I came in at the other. 'Hello stranger!' he called and came up to shake hands, twenty years having passed since our last meeting. And then with a sly grin he added, 'So now you've turned your nursery into a plant factory, I hear.' That remark made me wince, and my immediate reaction was to explain that if this was his impression I was sorry, but in any case what changes had taken place at Bressingham were not of my making.

Since then, further changes have come about. Perhaps further developments would be a more appropriate way to describe what my sons Adrian and Robert have brought about as I have taken more of a back seat. Adrian, 14 months younger than Robert, has been the one to make most of the openings by widening the range of plants and seizing every opportunity both for increased production and sales. He has been the one to nose out new introductions wherever they were to be found, in Japan, New Zealand and America, as well as in Europe, for he has a gift for spotting good plants. He also has a flair for giving them the requisite publicity. Yet for all his acumen, he manages to keep a balance between business considerations and a genuine love of plants.

Robert has willingly taken on many extra responsibilities concomit-ant with Adrian's drive for expansion. He is a 'nuts and bolts' man and has taken some intensive courses in business management. His main concerns are with finance, mechanisation, analysing costs and labour effectiveness, and he goes all out to inspire those in subordinate positions to willingly give of their best. To this end he calls regular staff meetings at more than one level and keeps all concerned in the know about how things are faring. Both he and Adrian pay a good deal of attention to staff welfare, including the provision of comfortable working conditions, so far as it is possible, in stark contrast to what I was able to achieve in former days. Whether output is commensurate with the improved working conditions is open to doubt (which I try to keep to myself), but I applaud their efforts to provide incentive. The climate and requirements of staff welfare has changed a lot over the past thirty years or so. There was no imposed necessity to foster a 'Bloom's News' of interest to the staff, nor to distribute Christmas hampers to the thirty or so employees who have now retired, or put on a fully subsidised party at Christmas for the 200 plus who have not – all this is due to Robert and Adrian's conscientious concern.

This could be one defence against any charge that the nursery has become a plant factory. It is true that there are assembly lines of a sort. To see four or five people round a potting machine might give that impression, but not so when seeing the way manual skill is employed for propagating and planting, even if the latter also takes the form of five people sitting on a tractor-hauled planter. There are now nine or ten full-sized tractors in place of the one tractor and two horses of the early 1950s. And there are even more than this number of small tractors which scurry around hauling trailers loaded with trays of plants to and from the production unit of 14,000 sq ft – in place of the chicken hut I had to use in 1947, and the back kitchen of my house. Office accommodation is far larger than the packing shed I built in 1948, and in the new packing shed up to a score of people work methodically during the order-lifting season.

My annual wholesale catalogue of 4,000 copies used to cost a few hundred pounds to print, but now the total annual cost of two retail catalogues and one wholesale catalogue is around £200,000, for the 100,000 or so copies printed. And, although colour illustrations are the heaviest charge, the catalogues now offer not only perennials and alpines, but conifers, heathers, ferns, shrubs and so on to double the content to about 3,000 items. Retail business inevitably calls for more staffing and more paper work. The wider the variety grown for sale the more difficult stock control becomes, and the more vital a part is played by the computer. I make a bit of a joke out of Robert's belief in the necessity of investing heavily in a computer. He said then that it was the only alternative to more office space and staff, but within, it seemed, only a year or two, several extra staff were taken on to meet the demands of the computer. The fact was, of course, that the business had expanded rapidly during that time. But that expansion has also resulted in the computer becoming something of a Moloch in its demands, involving the services of several people to justify its existence.

Such comments and statistics are only indirectly linked to Percy Picton's barbed remark. It pricked me because I knew what he was getting at, and it wasn't merely a tilt at our having expanded to some extent by adopting factory methods of mass production. Ever since expansion took off in 1970, a fear grew at the back of my mind that the personal, caring touch I had always enjoyed giving customers would give way to loss of intimacy and goodwill. This could come about even if standards of quality were maintained, because of a harder, more impersonal attitude which could well supervene on purely economic grounds. And indeed there is evidence of this happening wherever the jackboot of big business treads on older, gentler producer-purchaser relationships. My fear in other words was that in its growing large and strong the business would lose its 'soul'.

Although this fear remains, because the business is still growing, I should dismiss it in the face of so much evidence that neither Robert nor Adrian is the kind of man who wants to lose the personal touch. Their hearts and principles are in the right place, and just as they do more for the staff than they are obliged to in terms of welfare and involvement, so they study customer service. My wife Flora has, in fact, taken over the correspondence, sometimes involving a hundred letters a week, apart from telephone calls to answer queries and to ensure as far as is humanly possible that no customer remains dissatisfied, although complaints are rare. On the wholesale side, too, the same attitude prevails, and Lawrence Flatman with his 35 years experience with us likes to keep trade customers on the friendliest possible level.

It may be obvious that I have used Percy Picton's remark as a hook on which to air some information about the way in which our nurseries are run. And to conclude these explanations I should add that I felt no resentment at any aspersion he may or may not have implied, respecting and admiring him as I did for his opinions and vast knowledge of plants – and his generosity in sharing treasures. He took over the Colwall nursery from the redoubtable Ernest Ballard, who was also a hybridist of repute, expecially with Michaelmas daisies. He, too, was a plantsman like his friend Walter Ingwersen, who, with his son Will, make up a quartet who were, and in Will's case still are, plantsmen first and nurserymen second.

This combination is more likely to be evident in those who have retail nurseries. Retailing naturally appeals most to such plantsmen because connoisseurs among their amateur customers are attracted to the wide variety of plants they grow and offer arising from their love of plants. In my own case I resisted retailing for over thirty years, partly to avoid the extra detailed work involved, including exhibiting at shows. Another reason was to make it possible for other nurserymen to widen their range of the choicer, or less common plants, in the belief that perennials were undervalued as garden plants and that greater demand for them was there to be exploited.

Evidence that this was indeed the case came as a result of my garden being open to the public. As already mentioned, we had to give in to retail demand but only little by little because of our reluctance to tread on our retailing customers' preserves. When we began exhibiting at Chelsea again in 1965 and issuing an abridged retail catalogue, and on open days at Bressingham, there was a stall where visitors could buy a very limited selection of plants. To begin with it was mainly house plants and odds and ends, with no intention of direct sales of plants grown for wholesale customers on the nursery. But the stall became duplicated and expanded after a few years and offered a wider and wider variety of plants as visitors became more numerous and demanding.

When, in 1968, it dawned on me that a live steam museum was a worthwhile project, it never occurred to me that visitors' desire to purchase plants would be so great as to be irresistible. It built up as our retail section grew, backed by the colour catalogue and Chelsea exhibits – and, of course, by visitors' interest in my garden collection. With hindsight I now realise that when going all-out for the steam museum it would have been sensible to set up a comprehensive plant sales centre, too. When the need to correct this error of judgement became inescapable in 1984, we had a mere plot set aside for the sale of plants in the corner of the nearby little meadow, in which up to forty coaches could park on open days (still restricted to fifty occasions during the summer). Next to it was a seven-acre field which had been laid down to grass in 1969 as a car park for use on these open days.

It was with many misgivings that I agreed to a much larger cash-and-carry sales centre on that car park, so conveniently placed for the museum. But there was no other place it could go for it was also convenient for the nursery complex on the south side of the main highway. A rush job began early in 1985 and three acres were laid out with beds and benches on a hard surface. As a layout it was spacious and as a business venture so successful as to neccessitate its enlargement in 1986. It had, I suppose, to go all the way to make it attractive, even to the extent of providing refreshments, a book shop, and a children's play area.

It is not, we insist, a garden centre in the usual meaning of the term. It will not sell gnomes and ornaments, hammocks and garden furniture, and that's why it is called a Plant Centre. As such it probably has on display a wider variety of plants, shrubs and so on than any garden centre in the United Kingdom, but if anyone comes expecting to find every kind we grow and catalogue they will be disappointed. That would be virtually impossible for both economic and practical reasons, for not every kind lends itself to being containerised. Nor, for those who run it will there be freedom from worries, from the risk of losses from wind and weather and from pilfering. And in admitting that I should have sanctioned such a development years ago I can but give it my blessing now, even if it takes a few years to recover the high investment outlay. I am likely to remain a very infrequent visitor, but, well out of the way, I take some pleasure in potting-up unusual plants for them from my garden area.

Those in charge of the plant centre are a friendly little bunch and they sometimes seek my advice or come to see what I have potted for them to sell. It pleases them to see something out of the ordinary, as it does me to note their interest. I am willing enough to tell them all I know about this and that, the kind of information they would pass on to a customer to ensure its success in their garden, as they try to help the less knowledgeable. So often garden centres are staffed by assistants who have very little knowledge of what they sell, but not so with Tony Fry and his helpers. It pleases me to note such a caring attitude.

My aversion to being a salesman has not changed over the years. Perhaps it began in boyhood days when for several weeks between the New Year and late spring, Saturdays were spent hawking mustard and cress round the villages to earn a penny in the shilling. Then, my aim was parental approval. It was mostly self imposed for my father never complained if I did not sell all he sent me off with, knowing that I had tried. On one occasion it became dark when I was in the next village three miles from home, with still three or four unsold bags of cress to sell. Father became worried not knowing where I was and sent the village 'crier' out for me. I was on the way home and heard the crier's bell and raucous voice, and just then Father spotted me in the light cast by his bicycle lamp, carrying two empty basket trays. His relief and commendations, with a shiny sixpence to add to the pence I had fairly earned, was a great reward.

If I were to make a U-turn in my attitude to salesmanship, I doubt if the management would find me an asset. For one thing present-day prices due to inflation are hard to accept. I am well aware that this is being unrealistic when I know that wages alone are more than double in pounds per hour than what was paid for a week of fifty hours work less than fifty years ago. I know, too, that the selling price of plants has advanced by much less in proportion – at £1 for what used to be retailed for 9 pence in the old currency. There must be some kind of obstacle in my brain which refuses to accept such changes for I often find myself dividing present-day costs by some figure between ten and twenty in order to relate value to the time when there was a stable currency. This affects what I have to buy as well as what we produce to sell. Sometimes when plants I have reared come into the catalogue for the first time, I suggest the price tag, only to be told it is too low to be economic.

What they say I fail to take full account of is overheads and unseen costs of production. I am told that it costs about £30 to include a plant in the catalogue, and that even if only a hundred are grown for sale there is no profit margin unless more than half are sold. Such estimates, and I cannot dispute them, are a serious handicap to our policy of growing and offering the widest possible range of plants and I find it an unwelcome deterrent to my pleasurable role of making some good but neglected plants available to the public. A colour picture in the catalogue usually makes an enormous difference to sales but it is still a gamble, and ten times as many plants as normal have to be available of plants so illustrated.

In the simpler wholesale-only years, stocks of plants were geared to sales on a year to year basis. It was fairly safe to step up by say, ten per cent for next year what had sold well this year. Cutting down on stocks of a plant came only after sales had lagged for two seasons, for, even with wholesale, demand was somewhat fickle. And with field or container-grown perennials a carry over of unsold stock is uneconomic and a nuisance, with plants becoming either too large, or, if container grown, unthrifty because of confinement in a peat-based compost. This compost I do not like. It lacks body and staying power but it is used widely nowadays because it is light in weight, easy to handle and weed free – apart from liverwort and moss which make a harmful film after a time.

As a compromise I use up to half (by volume) sterilised loam in the compost used for the potting of plants for the Plant Centre. For years I have been advocating a loam content for the main nursery production which turn out several million on their potting machines. The argument against it has been the cost in labour of shredding and sterilising loam. The Royer Shredder and the flame-throwing steriliser have for long stood idle because of this, but at last the nursery is once more using a proportion of loam – but, for economic reasons, purchased in bags rather than using our own. One other indication of how labour costs have become such a bogey is that it is more economic to buy new plastic pots than to save, clean and use again those in which plants have died or become unsaleable. They are pitched out into huge skips to be taken away with other rubbish for disposal.

Here my old fashioned notions, likes and dislikes crop up again. I believe plants do better in clay pots because they have better porosity and drainage than plastic ones. Of the half million or so little pots in which alpines were grown by us until the 1950s, scarcely any are left. They somehow disappeared and broken ones were never replaced. But again I have to give in and admit that plastic pots are infinitely easier to use with their lightness and general convenience; and the Plant Centre could scarcely operate if clay pots were used.

Container-grown plants are more costly to produce than 'bare root' or 'field grown' plants, to use nurserymen's terms. This applies even where a planting machine is used, but not, of course, to alpines or rock garden plants which are too small for open ground production and need to be grown in pots in any case. The extra cost of containerising perennials and shrubs has to be passed on to the ultimate purchaser, but final satisfaction is by no means assured. What gardeners are paying extra for is the opportunity to make 'on sight' purchases, and very often at times of year when it would not be safe to move plants from the open ground into their gardens. It allows, too, for impulsive buying, especially strong when the plants are seen in bud and flower. This has undoubtedly led to a sales increase which would not have come about otherwise.

It is no wonder, therefore, that in the past twenty years or so garden centres have proliferated, to cater for a demand which scarcely existed before. It has to a large extent kept pace with the increase in the number of car owners, enabling more garden owners to become more mobile and garden conscious. Enthusiastic amateur gardeners may pore over catalogues, especially those in colour, but it is still more troublesome to write off for plants than to visit a local garden centre.

Container-grown nursery stock has the advantage of being safe to move and plant at any season. But losses can still occur from two causes. One is neglect of watering in dry periods, accentuated if the plant has been grown in a peaty compost with its roots confined or 'pot bound'. The other is that the peaty stuff continues to shrink and congested roots are slow to make entry into garden soil unless some roots are opened out and given repeated waterings. And if a plant is bought and transplanted in flower, the expected display is apt to be very brief and disappointing. It is true that container-grown plants are sometimes larger than those lifted from open ground and may appear to be better value despite the higher price, but generally speaking, the larger the plant the greater the risks – or the more fussing it requires to get it going in the buyer's garden.

A 'good nurseryman's plant' is a term which only a nurseryman would understand. It applies to those plants which have a perennial appeal, especially to impulse buyers, but which lack stamina through susceptibility to winter damage or loss, or because they tend to flower themselves to death. Two examples are catmint (*Nepeta*) and *Lithospermum* 'Heavenly Blue'. Both have a long and profuse flowering period and though both are hardy, they become weak with age. The nepeta dislikes winter wet and the lithospermum becomes twiggy and sprawling, objecting also to lime in the soil. But both are vigorous when young and, knowing the appeal they have to amateurs, a canny nurseryman will grow sufficient quantity from cuttings year after year to meet such a steady demand. And who can blame him? As far back as 1924 the demand for nepeta was so much ahead of the supply that the then popular ditty 'Yes, we have no bananas' was parodied with 'Yes, we have no nepeta' by some of my workmates at Wallace's nursery in Tunbridge Wells.

CHAPTER SEVEN

The Spice of Life

If I were condemned to practise gardening in a small area – as so many are – I am quite sure that variety in plant terms would take precedence over display considerations. It would, of course, come hard after having five acres in which to indulge in both variety and display to be restricted to, say, one tenth of an acre. But whereas groups of each kind of plant consist now of a dozen to twenty specimens, I would probably be reduced to just one of a kind. Even so, some rank-growing subjects would have to be eschewed in favour of having as many as possible of those plants which, with their grace and beauty of form, make no pretensions of providing a feast for the eyes alone. It is the plants that do more for one's aesthetic appreciation which create the greatest and most lasting interest, and engender one's deepest joy.

This is not to decry those garden owners who set out to make a small plot as bright and showy as space allows. This kind of result can be achieved by growing bulbous plants and annuals or bedding plants such as most parks or urban authorities go in for when aiming for popular appeal. The latter might dismiss any suggestion of planting up a section to be of special interest to those who are more aesthetically minded, because of the appeal it would also have for pilferers. One hears of artful dodges indulged in by the latter who take a delight in privily transporting choice plants from gardens open to the public to their own. Strange how so many people consider it quite legitimate to steal plants, seeds or cuttings for their own purposes without stopping to reflect that it is, in fact, as much an offence as taking goods from a supermarket's shelves with no intention of paying.

It may be easier to avoid being caught pilfering in a garden, but theft is now so prevalent that some gardens insist on all possible receptacles being left at the entrance. At Bressingham we have not been greatly troubled by pilferers. Once a woman was caught red-handed and I made her replant the pieces she'd torn out back again into the ground – to the amusement of several onlookers. On another occasion a party of students from a horticultural institute were reported as having abused our hospitality. I followed them into their coach and demanded back what they had taken – or else I would call in the police. What came out of their pockets was of no great value, but I was angry enough to threaten their principal with a ban on his students for what I saw as a mean and reprehensible trick.

To return to the theme of growing a wide variety of plants in a small space, it is quite feasible to cultivate successfully a hundred or more different specimens and cultivars in twenty square yards of open space. I am, of course, thinking of perennials, and if, say, five yards by four was the limit available, then some discreet selection – no matter how plants were acquired – would be necessary and there would be space for only one of a kind. Some would be dwarf or slow growing and none would be invasive. Some errors of judgement would be almost inevitable but this is where some of the spice comes in. In the process of readjustment for height and spread, one's interest grows as knowledge of such matters is acquired. Perhaps a few will prove resentful enough of the soil or site to sulk or even die, but if they do one can be quite sure that others can be found which will happily take their place.

It is safe to say that upwards of a thousand distinct species and cultivars are in existence and more or less readily available. And there are a few enthusiasts here and there who have a thousand or more in a relatively small garden. I know of one such in the Lake District with more like two thousand growing on a steep, rocky slope in less than one-third of an acre, a fair amount of which is taken up by rocks, paths and steps. It was featured on television in 1986 to give abundant proof that where there's a will there's a way.

I firmly believe that gardening with variety as the prime objective offers tremendous scope in a number of directions, for those who feel inspired to venture deeply into the realm of plants. It would be of special appeal and benefit to those who, having retired, are in need of some absorbing, worthwhile interest. After years of working to the clock, or a regular routine of some other kind, retirement often comes as a shock to the system and to adapt is often quite a problem. To be thrown back entirely on one's own resources, with perhaps another twenty years of potentially active life ahead may leave very few choices open. The kind of gardening I am suggesting is the most likely to be rewarding for anyone who has already a taste or a leaning towards cultivating plants for beauty's sake.

There was never any intention of making this yet another advisory book, but one piece of advice I must give is on labelling. So few people when bringing unfamiliar plants into their garden do more than stick in the nurseryman's label beside the plant and leave it at that. The chances are that a year later it will have vanished – and the name, as likely as not, from the owner's mind as well. Assuming the name on the label was the proper botanical name and not a common or folk name, then there may possibly be some way of checking up through an invoice but the likelihood is that there will be no record at all. While admitting that to label all one's plants is a tedious business and that if labels are too prominent they can detract from the overall view, labelling is necessary on several counts. First and foremost some familiarity with the contents of a bed or garden is a sure way of stimulating and maintaining interest. Without knowledge of the names of plants in one's garden one is at a severe disadvantage and handicapped in many unsuspected ways.

A bed containing a limited variety of plants may have the names of these recorded in a notebook. This reminds me of two instances where notes were used instead of labels. One was at Lord Talbot de Malahide's garden just north of Dublin where there was quite a large unlabelled collection of perennials and shrubs. His Lordship showed us round carrying a very large notebook in which every subject was recorded, but time and time again he paused, greatly puzzled, because on being asked the name of something new to me he couldn't find it where it should be in the book – each bed or border having its own number or description. The other occasion was a private arboretum in central Sweden which I was being shown round where the owner experienced much difficulty in finding the names of plants when his memory became unsure. His notes were on single sheets much thumbed and bedraggled. If he had tied tags on his trees and shrubs all would have been well.

Labels which are inserted in the ground have some disadvantages. They need to go far enough into the ground to stay there and I have heard of blackbirds and magpies pulling them out. I also came across a father and son pulling them out in my garden and sticking them in again elsewhere, just for fun, as they explained. I happened to catch them when only a dozen or so had been changed, and, showing some anger backed by a threat of a wilful damage charge under the law, made them, under my direction, replace the labels where they belonged. The labels that both my son Adrian and I use are quite expensive, cut out of laminated plastic by a pantograph machine to show a white name on a black background. They are rivetted on to rustless metal stalks and are not unduly obtrusive. They are not without faults, however, for not only is the plastic brittle, but in time algae creeps in and obscures the name, calling for a detergent wash every few years. These labels are fairly standard in large gardens nowadays, but if I had a small garden in which a wide variety of plants were being grown, I would use tags which dangled from a stiff piece of wire with the end curved into a hook. Another method would be to have aluminium name tags with the words written in indelible ink or with a special label pencil, wired on to a flat metal strip. Or, if the strip itself were aluminium, to write the name on this. But whichever method is used, the label should be long enough to stick three or four inches into the soil.

White plastic labels are not good in terms of permanence, and they are obtrusive enough to be an eyesore. I would still, however, advise a notebook or a card index record. We have to use the latter system because of a frequent need to raid a given plant for seed or cuttings, and the tendency there is to move a particular plant to a fresh place if it is thought that it will grow better or look better elsewhere. Groups are lifted, divided and replanted with us much more often than would be the case in most gardens because, if the nursery runs short of stock, I help out if I can. It is true that there are some garden owners, well steeped in botanical names, who are able to locate or name any one of perhaps hundreds of kinds. Such expertise comes to those who not only love their plants, but work with and amongst them season by season. For those fortunate few, labels are unnecessary and the respect they gain is matched only by their personal joy and satisfaction.

One very seldom finds such people to be perfectionist in their attitude. More often they are inclined to deprecate their achievements, conscious as they are of what they still have to learn and the subjects they have failed to grow successfully. A true gardener is never satisfied in that sense with his or her achievements – nor needs to be.

In the past twenty years or so several once famous names in the nursery world have disappeared from the view of the gardening public. This is linked, one suspects, with the radical changes in growing practices and the ways nursery stock is offered for sale, with garden centres becoming the major sales outlet.

It is doubtful if any other type of business can compare with the nursery trade as a whole for new entrants and for the rate of fall-out, so easy is it for someone with sufficient land to begin selling plants as a sideline. A little local demand with a roadside stall, perhaps or just a notice at the gate offering surplus produce, is often the beginning of more effort to rear what sells most readily. Prices have to be attractively low, as they can be if such a business is a sideline, but quality and correct naming are apt to be secondary considerations. Some investment in equipment to widen the range may follow and success becomes a lure to further effort. A catalogue or list, some advertising and exhibits at shows brings in more orders until paid help becomes necessary. This is the point at which one may be entitled to trade status, but it is also the point at which one begins to realise how exacting a profession it is. Such a realisation has led many a person to give it up as not worth the trouble and worry.

There is no doubt that the greater the variety of plants grown for sale, the more problems there will be to cope with, and the less likelihood of making commensurate profits. This can be said from my own experience, and other plant-loving nurserymen who have a personal delight in growing a large variety of subjects would agree. One cannot it seems, have it both ways, and although a rational middle way is possible, the collecting urge is well-nigh irresistible. Had I set my sights first and foremost on making profits I am quite sure that by growing large quantities of about a hundred or so popular kinds, whether for the wholesale or the retail market, I for one would have been far wealthier in money terms. This is what I would have been forced to do had my sons not come into the business.

Upon reflection I realise how fortunate I have been to survive as a nurseryman, despite the wide variety of plants which we grow commercially, when so many have been obliged to change direction or have gone out of business. Nowadays, after sixty years as a nurseryman, I can thankfully say that I am as much a collector as ever. Each year brings many more acquisitions from all over the temperate world to add to the 5,000 species and varieties I grow in my garden already, for whenever I visit other specialist gardens I find something to note and, hopefully, to swop. A fairly recent trip to Sweden added about seventy to the list, but sadly only a few of them have come into the garden. My son Adrian, as already indicated, gets around much more than I do and as many or more new plants come from his peregrinations – and he is just as keen as I am on collecting. And, whereas I stick to perennials and alpines, his roving eye takes in hardwood subjects as well.

Collecting and exchanging plants with others is the most productive means of adding variety to one's garden. One is constantly surprised at the number of kinds in existence somewhere or other which one has never heard of. There was a time when, fascinated with the vast numbers of species in the seed lists of some botanic gardens, I fell for the temptation to try some with no idea of how they would turn out when reared. Such lists do not give descriptions, nor do they make distinctions between annuals and perennials, hard or soft wooded plants, weeds or worthy plants. They are listed under their botanical family headings, and, in making a selection, I was guided merely by the sound or the indication provided by the meaning of the plant's specific name, not all of which I could decipher.

This was a phase which lasted only a year or two, for, when some from the first batch of seeds, from Moscow Botanic Garden, turned out to be either weedy, worthless or merely annuals of no garden merit, I saw the folly of it. It would have been more sensible to go to Moscow and see for myself, for this could have resulted in some worthwhile additions. As it was, from that batch of seed packets, one single plant was worth going on with. It was the only seed to germinate of *Polygonum regelianum*, which, being named in honour of a famous botanist, became a dozen attractive plants as a garden group by simple division. After a few more years, sales through the retail catalogue were proving that I was not alone in my estimation of its garden value. It sets very little seed and division of the hefty clumps is not easy because of its tendency to make very few shoots coming from its clumpy, fleshy rootstock, and these come not at the top but from underneath. From among the few seedlings we have been able to raise there appeared one with much deeper, bright pink, bottle-brush spikes. And all being well, this will be given a cultivar name once in sufficient supply to meet an expected demand.

Natural breaks, variation and hybrids are not common, but they do occur especially when a wide range of plants is grown. Two such, *Potentilla* 'Flamenco' and *Mertensia* 'Blue Drop', have appeared as self-sown seedlings, but this is a rare occurrence and after a few years of struggle to propagate the mertensia it died out from, I guess, sheer resentment. Several of the improved cultivars have occurred without first receiving Percy Piper's 'fiddling' by way of encouragement. A species with some natural tendency to show variations from seed has been another source, but seed from an existing cultivar is even more likely to yield one or two worthwhile variations.

A deliberate cross between two species is very chancy, but between two cultivars – the method practised by specialists in a popular genus such as roses – remains the most reliable and most practical method of hybridising. Secretly, I hope it will always be thus, but great strides have been made in recent years in the field of biotechnology by which the genetic changes of a given subject are the result of radiation to produce mutations. A consortium has been formed, of which my son Robert has been elected chairman, to take up this new challenge under laboratory conditions. Its object is, of course, to produce new plants and shrubs by modern intensive methods, which, in the fullness of time, will be launched as novelties on to the gardening market. It has great possibilities, but I am old-fashioned enough to have doubts and misgivings, not so much in respect of a reluctance on moral grounds to tamper with nature to this extent, as to eliminate the gentler craft of hybridising by traditional means. Most people who are able to look back over many years are prone to have ambivalent feelings about the changes they have witnessed. They are not likely to see all these changes as progress in the right direction, whereas younger folk are inclined to do so – and to grasp any advantage they offer. But in some cases progress is made at some cost, with not much evidence to be seen of it enabling people to live more wholesome lives as individuals, to live fully and purposefully.

There seems to be an aggressive element in many areas of research towards the exploitation of natural resources, and the hitherto unsuspected means of opening up secrets by such means as biochemistry. Unknown risks are being courted in attempting to conquer anything which offers more wealth and status to the so-called Lords of Creation. But it brings to mind for some of us a profound statement made nearly 2,000 years ago – 'What shall it profit man if he gains the whole world and loses his own soul?'

This reflection comes to mind when considering the possible effect of modern technology – quite apart from labour saving machines and so on – on the gentle art of gardening. If, in the future, for example, hybridising is to move into the realm of the boffins and the laboratory, the would-be hybridist who dabbles (or 'fiddles') because of a love for plants may well lose the incentive to continue, and so this may join so many other skills and crafts which have been lost in the name of progress.

One wonders sometimes what is the true motivation of those who are the spearhead of this kind of progress – the kind that eliminates individual skills. This is where my own ambivalence comes into question. The consortium of nurserymen who are backing the new development referred to are hoping for profit-making results. Such motivation affects the technicians in the laboratory as well, and I would be scorned if I attempted to hinder them. Maybe it is a case of 'if you can't lick them, join them'.

This new approach to hybridising is only just taking shape. But micro-propagation or tissue culture is now a fact of life for nurserymen. As a development in rapid propagation it is truly weird and wonderful to produce thousands and thousands of tiny plants by this means in a matter of months from a piece of plant tissue. It is by way of being a discovery rather than a new invention, unlike using radiation to make a plant mutate. Nor does it appear to hold the element of danger which the use of radiation would suggest. Tissue culture is enticing a plant to respond to a process of increase which must be inherent in its nature, though by no means all plants will respond. Some that do but are liable to a virus infection have produced offspring which are perfectly healthy, although this is not to say that they will remain immune.

Having enjoyed propagating as a rewarding and essential part of my working life, I can but hope that there will always be some plants which fail to reproduce by tissue culture. But several instances have already occurred of word coming through to me from the nursery that there is no need to take cuttings or divisions of certain plants because a large batch of tissue-raised plants is on the way. All I can do is to accept the change with good grace, with the reflection that the nursery business may benefit and, ultimately, the customer, and that so far as I can foresee there is no likelihood of me being made redundant as a propagator during my lifetime.

CHAPTER EIGHT

Motivations

There are only three helpers still around who have been with me since the old days. With a few reservations we all agree that there was a lot to be said for them. Alf Kester was the only one to come to Bressingham from Oakington – apart from Len Smith who stayed only a year because his wife became homesick. Alf began on leaving school in 1926 and now in his retirement still works part time. Percy Piper is another retired old timer. But Don Hubbard switched from being nursery lorry driver, package sealer and irrigation pipe layer to become the steam museum painter. We are all inclined to hark back, not to call them 'the good old days' with unalloyed nostalgia, but to pick out times when nursery work, despite somewhat harsh conditions, was more satisfying than seems now to be the case. We agree that what people never had they never missed. But now some workers are less satisfied in spite of having so much more money to spend, and more time away from work in which to spend it.

If we old timers are apt to forget the hard times and remember what we found satisfying, we are also apt to be somewhat scathing of the approach of so many nowadays to work. To do as little as possible for as much as one can get is a widespread attitude. In our life-time almost, it has gone from one extreme to the other – along with inflation, for the latter goes inevitably with a higher standard of living. A lifetime ago, slackers were simply not tolerated, and, if some employers took undue advantage of their rights, the effect of two world wars and of labour becoming more organised has brought an almost reversed situation. The one who pays the piper can no longer freely call the tune, and the happy medium between the two has yet to be found. The Japanese who are closest to achieving good employer–worker relationships are also well on the way to being the most prosperous nation on earth.

Prosperity, however, is not, or should not be, the sole aim in life. So often the urge to seek prosperity brings out what I believe is the most damaging of human weaknesses, namely greed. And almost always those with much want more. Greed was much in evidence during the period of Britain's greatness as a world leader in empire building and industry. But that kind of prosperity and influence was dependent on the majority of people working long hours at bare subsistence wages. As the standard of living improved for them, so industrial output declined and inflation set in. As social security, along with union power, whittled down the individual incentive to work, so more and more people got the idea that the State owes them a living. And greed still flourishes among those with the means to practise it, and this still results in, I believe, about 10 per cent of the population holding 90 per cent of the nation's wealth, which is not to say that only they have been greedy. Far from it, because it is the weakness of so many of us to fail to distinguish between our needs and our greeds.

Generalisations are mostly rather vapid and the above may be no exception. I must also confess to being one of those people who, if they sometimes give expression to some fundamental beliefs and criticisms, do little or nothing by way of righting what they see as wrongs. I can, for example, believe fervently that peaceful co-existence between all mankind is the ideal state in which human creative potential can flourish, but I shy away from actively campaigning for peace.

I find it somewhat embarrassing to be told that some of the things I have done creatively, or written out of conviction, have been an inspiration to others. Such remarks prick my conscience. They make me realise how much more I could have done in life had I not been so often at odds with myself. But now that I have largely come to terms with myself, and have a greater understanding of what makes me 'tick', the true pattern of the past 70 years has become clarified. Some of my deviations, for example, can be seen now as sublimations to urges I failed to comprehend at the time.

My deviation into preserving steam engines may or may not be correctly placed in this context. It came from a very different impulse to that which pushed me into land reclamation at Burwell, or making a large garden and lake. These last had some direct connection with my work as a landsman, but, although lacking in engineering skill, steam engines had appealed to me ever since I was a toddler. I became the proud owner of a traction engine in 1947 and mourned its loss when I found it had been destroyed for scrap during my stay in Canada. Several years passed before I felt able to spare the money or the time to replace it, and then when I did I found I was not content with just one. By the end of 1961 I had nine and a year later, fourteen. All these were road-using engines, and, still not satisfied, I went on to collect rail-using and industrial stationary engines until the number passed fifty, including some on permanent loan.

As with other projects I have engaged in, I needed to be fully involved with the work of restoration. With skilled help offered for the mechanical side, I enjoyed scraping off rust and grime and applying the many coats of paint necessary to preserve and give these engines back their pride, working often until late on winter nights in a cold, draughty shed. Each new arrival was a thrill, as it was when another old timer came to life again. One or two of my gardening acquaintances made sly remarks about my priorities having switched from plants to engines. Knowing this to be partially true only when the plants needed less of my attention, I reacted with some vigour, but gradually the restoration work was passed on to others as impetus towards the creation of a proper museum gained strength.

There was, I believed, some merit in accumulating a collection of old engines if only because visitors to the garden on open days increased with them on display, at a time when gate receipts were donated to charities. There was a pretty good excuse also to go in for narrow gauge railways, to enable visitors to view the nursery from a train and pay fares which would go towards the restoration and maintenance costs. It was not until 1968 when the chance came to have an ex British Railways locomotive on permanent loan that the idea of a comprehensive live-steam museum occurred to me. The need existed and that we had the scope. The emphasis on live steam was paramount in ensuring the museum's success. And then it became essential to form a charitable trust to ensure its long-term future.

As Chairman of the Trust and Director of the Museum I could not be otherwise than deeply involved. But as, over the years, a permanent staff has taken over more and more of the maintenance, repair and administration, so I have been glad to let them do it. I enjoy driving a two-foot gauge locomotive hauling its train on the two-and-a-quarter-mile Nursery Line on open days. Over a complete season it amounts to between 600 and 700 trips and, when busy, a dozen to fifteen trips in one day amounts to that number multiplied by hundreds of passengers. My only skill as an engineman is to keep a good head of steam by the discreet use of coal and water, and to see that the moving parts are kept well oiled. But when occasionally I am asked which is my first love, engines or gardening, I can truthfully reply that steam is no more than a hobby, a trifle overgrown though it may be. And during the six months between September and April over 90 per cent of my time is spent with plants.

Nothing stands still for long either with engines or plants with regard to the part both play in what I suppose could be termed the Bressingham complex. Even a static engine is subject to its boiler being slowly, insidiously weakened by internal rusting, a part which will eventually have to be replaced at enormous cost if ever it is to become active again. There are already renewals to be made on our five miles of railway track and this will be an ongoing expense. A now obsolete size of some essential fitting will cost up to £100 for what could have been bought for £1 when steam engines were commonplace. And in 1985 it cost almost £1,000 just to have the asbestos lagging removed from a relatively small locomotive boiler before it could be officially inspected under the Health and Safety rules in order to renew insurance cover.

So much for the gloomy side of the future prospects for the Steam Museum. Its proximity has made a considerable impact on the new retail plant centre. The influx of visitors when both museum and gardens are open boost sales enormously. But the plant centre is open every day from 9.30 a.m. to 5.30 p.m., and there the problem for the museum begins. As a live steam museum it can only operate economically if a considerable number of people come to take rides on the railways and the steam roundabouts, as well as to see the garden. Both open days and hours have therefore to be limited, and we have no wish to have a trickle of visitors in either the garden or the museum area which would inevitably be distracting for those at work in both places. Plant-centre visitors coming from a distance may be annoyed if told the museum and gardens are closed except on the 50 specified days. But for all the benefit these twin attractions are to the plant centre, those dual-intent visitors may become an intolerable nuisance.

This is just another example of how secondary issues are apt to emerge unexpectedly from what, at first, appears to be a simple, straight-forward concept. And, as I hark back 25 years to the time when I bought an old traction engine as a pet hobby, it emphasises once again how an impulse or decision can lead to unimaginable consequences affecting other people in the process. My count of years is conducive to retrospection sometimes, and my work to introspection. The power of objective thinking has always eluded me, and although I spend many hours on repetitive jobs – such as propagating, potting, hoeing, digging and planting – my mind seems to hover between trivial thoughts or reflections and concentration on the work in hand.

It requires objective thinking to decide how I am to accomplish what I am doing by the quickest and least arduous means possible, taking account always of the welfare of the plant I happen to be concerned with at that time and commercial stock requirements. Such circumstances are not a good seed bed for any uplifting or inspirational thoughts, but, although I like to believe I'm still a seeker after truth and wholeness of living, I am pretty certain I shall find these as much of a will o'the wisp as achieving perfection in my gardening enterprises.

In 1984 BBC producer John Kenyon came up with the idea of making a series of programmes entitled 'The Mavericks', and asked me to be the subject of the first one. I was also asked to be on Radio 4's weekly profile. To be considered a maverick is much the same thing as being an eccentric, and at odd times I have pondered whether or not I belong to such a category. Not that I find it at all offensive.

The suggestion that I am a maverick or eccentric is somewhat amusing, especially as so much effort on my part was directed when I was younger to conforming to the accepted social pattern. In my young days the odds were very much against anyone who attempted to express their individuality beyond a certain very limited degree. You were commended for being a hard worker, for having a keen eye for business, for prowess at sport and for regular church attendance, but to be unconventional was to put you on a par with a drunkard or a ne'er-do-well, or an aloof intellectual. So when, as a small boy, I felt urges to do or be what boys are not supposed to do or be, if they wished to grow up into respectable manhood, I had to pretend so hard I was just like other boys that this aim became in itself a worthy objective to pursue.

The break away from conventional attire and behaviour among young people is a modern phenomenon. They would not have been tolerated sixty years ago as they are nowadays. As a rebellion against conformity it runs counter to the older, deep-seated urge to become integrated in society from infancy to adulthood. This is what I tried to but never succeeded entirely in doing, and, as a consequence, I was often subject to inner conflict as a result of trying to suppress my brand of individuality. It could well be that some of my more outlandish projects were by way of sublimation. One of the compensations of increasing age has for me been a diminishing concern for what other people might think. I objected as a very small boy, for example, to having my hair cut for the first time. Not that I wanted to appear girlish, but I saw no good reason for it being shorn. This aversion persisted, supported often by the knowledge that in times past men wore long hair more often than short. But over sixty years passed before I found the courage to defy convention, during which time I came to loathe the interior of hairdressing salons. At about nine years of age a longing came to wear earrings and I could see no reason why I shouldn't – except that I knew I would not be allowed to do so. A very few elderly men did in those days and it was believed those little gold rings improved eyesight. Again, the longing never left me and again I finally gave in to it, but not in public until I reached seventy, and then I chose silver ones to match my hair.

Those who give me sideways glances because of my appearance may imagine I wear long hair and earrings as an adornment – or to draw attention to myself. But they are entirely wrong in this respect. I do not doubt that there is a psychological explanation, but see no need to explore it in this context. Suffice it to say that in this outward expression of peculiar longings long suppressed it became a contributing factor to what sense of wholeness of personality I have achieved. What others may deduce is now of no concern to me. If such harmless expressions are indicative of being a maverick or an eccentric, it does not bother me. I am not aware of having lost any friends, but in the twelve years since I kicked over the traces of convention I can think of several I have gained who accept me – warts an'all.

The great majority of my friendships have been made through the medium of plants. They include some Americans as a result of a spate of lecturing trips I have made to the United States in the past seven years. I was given invitations long before that but shirked the hassle and the journey. Having at last made the effort I found such warmth and interest in my speciality as to go again and again to speak to both east- and west-coast enthusiasts. American gardeners hold English gardens and gardeners in such high regard that many come over each year almost as pilgrims. And now that their interest has recently become focussed on perennials it brushes off on me.

One newspaper report of a talk I gave dubbed me in a caption as 'The Guru of Perennials', more an example of the Americans' tendency to overstate than a statement of fact. Not that the British are much less flamboyant in their verbiage. Even Percy Thrower, for instance, must surely have squirmed when he found himself referred to as 'The Nation's Head Gardener' by the press, or when, in a woman's romantic fiction story, the author referred to her heroine as 'feeling as safe in his arms as a tender seedling in the hands of Percy Thrower'. The fact is that those of us who are arbitrarily quoted as being experts tend to avoid our ignorance showing up in public – a tendency practised as a matter of course by professionals in any sphere. Some of us are deeply conscious of what we do not know and with age realise more and more what knowledge will be beyond our capacity to acquire. Some of my gardening friends and acquaintances have a wider knowledge than I possess. But they lack, unfortunately, the incentive to put it on record. This impression comes from talking with such as Maurice Mason, Fred Barcock (a Suffolk nurseryman), Valerie Finnis and Percy Picton. But those of us who write books and articles or give lectures and become well known are given accolades which are not perhaps wholly deserved. Not that we should cavil or go in for mock modesty since what we say or write is lapped up as useful by those avid for gardening information. There is no mystique about being a writer. Motivations vary all the way from those with a compulsive urge to pass on what they have learned to those who seek profit or kudos, whether or not they write from personal experience. The latter have plenty of the former's experience to draw from and it is easy enough for plagiarists to convey the impression of being authorities.

It is probably a weakness on my part to prefer being goaded from within, and to want to be fully occupied mentally and physically. This has been pretty constant throughout my life and what dread I have of the incapacities of old age centre on this theme. One aspect of this urge is to rush in to a project with too little forethought and planning, too little attention to detail in the process of working towards a given end. Not that I deliberately skimp, but rather that my absorption tends to cloud the overall vision instead of taking full account of all the factors with analytical precision and diligence.

Having made this confession and engaged in the writing of this book as a result of a compulsive urge, I come back to existing realities. First and foremost is the awareness of my good fortune in having chosen to become a nurserymen, coupled with the incentive to live fully, and to be sustained so far with good health. Obviously I have no reason to doubt the link existing between interesting work and robust health. But I also like to believe that my work being centred on plants, this too has played a vital part. For much of the winter the perennials on which I exercise what skills I possess are fully alive but resting, waiting for spring warmth and sunshine to bring them back to growth and beauty. My manipulations are designed to multiply their potential as individuals and to widen their appeal, and in this, surely, there is an element of love, as well as of faith and hope, with which or by which I can feel some kinship and identity. They will outlive me, but in being so closely associated with them as a temporary custodian, it is possible to glimpse fleeting intimations of immortality.

CHAPTER NINE

Weeds in Context

Weeds have been glibly defined as plants in the wrong place. Such an aphorism may have first been coined by some gardener of repute wanting to impress an audience avid for words of wisdom, witty maybe, but totally inadequate and yet too all-embracing at one and the same time. For example, it turns a six-foot delphinium into a weed if, by some error, it turns up in a rock garden. It is not enough to declare that common weeds occuring amongst plants grown for their interest or decorative effect are plants in the wrong place. True, any weed is a plant in its own right. It has a botanical name and, in that sense at least, is on a par with the choicest decorative species. If the dandelion, *Taraxacum officinale*, for instance, did not seed itself around, its bright yellow flowers and fluffy seed heads would make it a good garden plant instead of being such a nuisance.

For a long time people were led to believe that weeds were sent along with God's curse on Adam in the Garden of Eden. As a result, Adam had to work and sweat as a gardener in order to eat, with a little to spare for Eve no doubt. But the weeds were there long before Adam became a gardener, although, as allegory, the story has a certain richness as well as some messages for us today. What Adam saw as weeds were plants with no food value, and, if he appreciated those having beauty enough not to harm them, then he had begun to realise that man could not live by bread alone. What he would not have considered was that the growth he hacked out as weeds, had a right to be there in the natural order of things.

This is a fact which it is as well for us to realise, too, even if some of our common weeds are foreigners who have been given the chance, mostly by human agency, to invade and prosper because of their adaptability. These are no less deserving of respect in the widest sense, for, if all weeds are enemies in the gardener's eyes, they are nevertheless an integral part of nature.

We gardeners seldom bother to observe the processes by which nature takes over a plot or piece of land which has been neglected or devastated. Some plant growth will appear even where there would appear to be no fertility whatever. It may take years before perennials, grass, weeds, shrubs or trees colonise it completely, but the law of survival of the fittest sees colonisation completed sooner or later. In a neglected garden this takes place much quicker than on an arid plot. In a matter of weeks a spick and span garden can be an unholy tangle with weeds competing with plants for light and nutriment, presenting a daunting task to the would-be rescuer.

Just as perennials eventually dominate a wholly neglected plot, so they will do the same in a neglected garden. It is these perennial weeds that are the greatest menace to gardeners, for however thickly annual weeds come up, they can be killed off provided the slaughter with a hoe begins while they are tiny. The best time of all for a quick, easy kill of these is when they are almost too small to see. This applies to perennial weeds, too, if they are seedlings, as usually they are mixed in with the annuals. Most garden soils contain enough viable weed seeds, just waiting for the chance to germinate, to produce a fresh crop of seedlings every time the soil is turned over or even disturbed. 'One year's seeding is seven years weeding', is an adage worth remembering for it is true. Weeds such as groundsel can produce several generations in a single year if allowed to do so. Annual stinging nettles can produce and drop seeds all the year round, and lose little of their vitality whether on the surface or dug in to germinate at a future date. I have known deep digging to produce different kinds of weeds to those which have been growing on that particular piece of ground before, and I believe Darwin found some fifty different weeds came up from the soil he scraped from a shot pheasant's feet.

From the standpoint of a specialist in perennials and alpines, the case against using chemical weed-killers is overwhelming. Their use on a bare piece of ground is all right so long as instructions are followed. But where a bed or border is already planted, then it is not merely dangerous but less effective than hoeing, even if the plants are carefully masked or avoided. A contact weed-killer can be used over dormant leafless plants, but I find even then that it creates a film which inhibits aeration and needs to be stirred with a hoe within a few weeks. Some systemic weed-killers are designed to make a complete kill, and, even if they are reputed to be selective, it is seldom safe to use them where other plants are growing when the objective is to kill some deep-rooting perennial weed.

Which brings me to perennial weeds. One of these, the lesser celandine, I would not wish to eliminate, troublesome though it is in my garden. Its shiny, rounded, deep green leaves are a perfect complement to its cheerful yellow flowers in spring. If it were not a plant with such a nuisance value, I would want to grow it, or I would try to isolate it somewhere if I could for I would miss its welcome to spring. Usually I let it flower and then try to fork it out before seeding takes place. This is enough when it is growing between other plants, but well nigh impossible when it is established with its tiny, claw-like white roots in with some clumpy subject.

That said, I would hesitate to say which is the worst perennial weed I am at war with. Ground elder (bishop's weed), marestail (or horsetail) and the larger bindweed or bell vine are for me the most persistent and difficult to control. All in their various ways are insidious, pernicious and destructive. Ground elder is seldom killed by merely one dose of systemic weed-killer and will lurk in the rootstock of other plants or hard-wood growth ready to sally forth again. For this reason other remedies such as smothering with black polythene are also likely to be ineffective. The menace of marestail is its rapid spread from its black roots which delve so deep that no fork can ever reach them. I have known them to go under gravel paths and the foundations of walls to appear on the other side. It has no leaves to absorb a weed-killer effectively, but bruising or treading over the stems before treatment is helpful. To use a special impregnated glove may be the method to adopt for a small infestation, but spray after spray, may be year after year, where it is dense or widespread, usually works.

Bindweed is in much the same category as marestail. It has very deep and widely penetrating white roots and no amount of digging them out seems to reduce its vigour. This, too, will lurk in some permanent host.

My worst patch has its home base in an ancient honeysuckle, and time and again has spread out from there. It is leafy enough to take weed-killer and will quickly show its effects. But while strangling (as its tentacles do) the stems of other plants, one is apt to avoid giving a complete overall dosage, which would make a surer kill if repeated often enough.

Another quite pretty weed is oxalis. The plural should be used here for there are three of them. Not that any are common so far as I know, but they could become so. The clover-leaved species has occasional salmon-pink flowers only three to four inches tall. The tiny bulbous root is the real menace for it forms many bulblets which become detached and so enlarge an infestation rapidly. As it has a long dormant period from autumn to late spring, one is apt to overlook its malignant presence among other plants because, as already mentioned, it is quite pretty. So, too, is a little yellow-flowered creeping species which delights in insinuating itself among alpine plants. It is so diminutive in all its parts that, again, it may be overlooked and even admired for its tiny bright yellow flowers until it is too late to tease it away from a choice dianthus or saxifraga. The third is a larger, less invasive species, often with purplish leaves and larger yellow flowers. Its name is *Oxalis corniculata*, and, for all his antipathy towards bedding, William Robinson mentioned that it had some value for this purpose.

For many, the most malignant weed is couch-grass which also bears the name tweetch, wicks and speargrass, according to locality. In my experience it is not the worst of weeds, but it is among the worst when it finds a refuge or base camp within a clumpy perennial or the roots of other subjects. When that happens, then it is almost as bad as ground elder, and total eradication is unlikely unless there is total clearance to begin with. In a bare patch of ground, couch can be killed by chemicals if these are applied when there is ample greenery, but one has to wait weeks in case of revival before digging it out for replanting. This, I have found, is less effective than forking over the area in the first place, especially if one works with the weather. Couch is not deep rooting and if cast out with a shake on top, sun and wind will kill it more quickly than any chemical. And if the process has to be repeated once or twice more, it is a more satisfying job than having to witness its slow decay from poison.

A farmer years ago rather boastfully told me how he cleaned up a couch-infested field. He had bought it cheaply because it was so foul. It was during the depression of the 1920s and the previous owner had done no more than plough and harrow to sow barley year after year, shirking a summer fallow which might have cleaned it out. 'I gave it', said the new owner, 'a proper smothering of muck and ploughed it in with the couch. The next year all those little bits had grown strong and healthy instead of being starved like the land was. And then up it came with ploughing and pulling about until it was all on top, and, as soon as I could, I burnt it in dozens of little fires. Ash from burnt couch is good for the soil, and after that – well, I had crops like nobody had ever seen on that field before.' The point of this will not be missed. Perennial weeds such as couch are easier to master on soil of high fertility.

But there are at least three other creeping weeds to mention, namely creeping thistle, creeping cress and creeping sorrel. The most common of these is the creeping thistle, and in my experience the easiest of the three to control. It will weaken and die if chopped off as soon as it breaks surface, keeping at it to make it bleed to death all summer and continuing the process in the following spring, if it re-appears. A small patch is not much of a problem, but for a larger infestation a systemic weed-killer may have to be used, and this is very effective – one dose is usually enough. Not so with creeping cress which has some artful habits. A single plant with its deeply cut leaves and sprays of small yellow flowers may appear to be harmless and even pretty in its way. But left alone, if only for a month, it sends out thread-like shoots which spread to make a patch a yard or more across in one season. Its domain is deceptively wide and its roots are so thin and brittle that forking them out seldom gets them all. And if a systemic weed-killer is applied to the foliage only it does not always reach those insidious, outspreading roots. Nor will an application stop seeding if it is applied after flowering.

Creeping sorrel is of concern, I believe, only to those on neutral or acid soils, so an application of lime can be an inhibitor where weeding fails to clean the ground or where poison cannot be applied.

Let it not be thought that I am prejudiced against the use of chemical aids to combat weeds. It is just that, having had experience of them, I would revert to the time-honoured, healthful use of mind and muscle where proof exists that the best results come by this combination of effort. Over the past thirty or forty years labour-saving has become almost a watchword if not a fetish. Gardeners have collectively spent vast sums on implements, machines, as well as chemical concoctions carrying the labour-saving tag, often with very extravagant claims being made of their efficiency. But where weeds are concerned there are very few instances where such claims can be fully substantiated in practice. Contact weed-killers can keep areas between shrubs free of weeds, and in large gardens labour costs leave little alternative to their use. But a sour, arid, crusted soil resulting from repeated doses of such chemicals is not a pretty sight, nor is it conducive to aeration on which full fertility so much depends.

The presence of nettles and fat hen are said to indicate good soil. It would be safer to say 'potentially good soil', however, because on really fertile soil both will be at least double the height and have twice the vigour of those growing in places where fertility or moisture is lacking. Much the same applies to willow weed and the so-called nightshade. There is more than one species of willow weed which is seen most often on damper, peaty soils with branching, knotty stems and little clusters of pink flowers. Willow weed drops green viable seeds, as does the annual stinging nettle, but if it is late to germinate in May it forms spreading bushes several feet across by August. Nightshade is also bush forming with little white flowers and green berries which turn black on ripening. Its kinship with tomatoes and potatoes is easy to discern, and a mature plant may grow nearly a yard high and as much across, calling for considerable effort to get rid of it. When pulled up it is more likely to break apart at ground level than to come up, roots and all.

Fat hen – 'muck weed' as it is called in some parts – grows erectly, seldom forming any branches. Given the good moist soil it likes, it can attain a height of three to four feet, with glacous green foliage arising from a tough, woody stem, topped by a conical head of flowers scarcely recognisable as such and quickly followed by a profusion of greenish seeds. It takes a razor-sharp implement to sever the stem at ground level, but pulling out is a much easier task for it carries very little soil on the roots after shaking out. May weed has not been one of my afflictions, but I fancy it could be if left to seed ad. lib. Its forms mats of deep green, finely cut leaves and up-facing white daisy flowers come on three- to six-inch stems. For all its summer spread of up to a foot or more (but coming from a single root stem) the plant will soon shrivel if the stem is severed – with a sharp instrument, for it is pretty tough.

Fat hen, willow weed and nightshade are annuals, like the small, dark-leaved stinging nettle. The last-mentioned differs in habit from the other three in its ability to germinate and grow at any time of the year given sufficient warmth and moisture. Groundsel and chickweed are also in this category, and all have a great capacity for seeding. A soil surface cleaned of summer weeds to be spick and span in October may be a green carpet by spring, with an assortment of all of these and annual grass, with, maybe, a hundred little plants to every square foot. It is not difficult to dig over the ground again in March to leave it clean and ready for planting or sowing, but it is a sober reminder of the weed-seed content of the soil. Hopefully, too, it will leave one with a resolve not to use weed-killer when action with fork or spade does a far better job more quickly.

Chickweed, however, is almost in a class by itself. It is a short-lived perennial rather than an annual, because it often roots down as it spreads. And spread it will, especially in moist, fine soil. If left to flourish too long it will cling to the hoe and clog it up with its fine soil-holding roots, causing extreme annoyance and frustration. It wraps itself round other weeds and the plants one wishes to liberate from its clutches, and if the soil is damp one is inclined to feel desperate. In my time I have clawed it out with my bare hands, never leaving it lying on the ground to take root again as soon as my back is turned, but dumping it in a barrow and onto a heap for rotting down. Knowing that chickweed will grow and seed throughout the year except during frosty spells, tends to make one careful not to allow small seedlings to become expansive, as they undoubtedly will on fine soil in dampish weather. They even have the ability, once they get a hold (although the roots are not deep-penetrating), to keep the surface soil damp by shielding it from the drying effects of sun and wind.

Everyone, I imagine, knows how persistent the perennial stinging nettle can be – and how adaptable it is to very widely varying conditions. If it is growing in grass, a selective weed-killer will kill it, although a second application may be necessary. Before the era of weed-killing chemicals we used to slash and bruise them, but this had to be repeated time and time again to be effective. And nettles are so spiteful. Many a time I have attacked a dense bed with a scythe and a sense of guilt as well as hatred, having failed to tackle them in spring. By June, the stems rise four feet or more high, and, however artfully the scythe was wielded, there would be some which fell towards my bare arms and set up an eighteen-hour itch. Where nettles and nothing much else is growing, then a killer spray is a blessing. It needs to be applied first in April and then again in summer over any young, resurgent growth. But to dig out the roots wherever they are calls for an implacable hatred of the species, and grim determination to master it. Both fork and spade are required, as well as gloves, because nettles have a defiant streak in their nature, making them determined to hold on to the territory they have acquired as if it were theirs by right.

CHAPTER TEN

Long Answers to Short Questions

When asked, as sometimes I am, what is my favourite plant, it has a paralysing effect on my mind. I pause, hoping for a quick or direct answer to surface. But it never comes, because, as I have finally to admit, it depends on the time of year. From the long succession of flowering, from February to November, there is an equally long list of flowers for which I have a special affection. Each of them seem to epitomise their own season, especially those at the beginning and the end of the year when there is a smaller selection.

I am greatly attracted to the earliest plants to flower because they are the harbingers of spring, keeping faith from one year to another and poking through the cold, damp soil to delight the eye and raise the spirits anew. I am thinking here especially of *Adonis amurensis*, behaving just as it does at home in eastern Siberia by being the first truly herbaceous plant to brave the elements in February, or even January when the weather is mild. It is a fibrous-rooted plant with small, tight crown shoots and its greenish-yellow often shows up in the bud stage in January, at much the same time as its relative the winter aconite. It has a similarly shaped flower to the latter and though the yellow glistens, the hint of green remains, though not so marked as in the double-flowered form. The double 'plena' comes two or three weeks later than the single, always with leaves appearing as the buds begin to open. As the flowers fade, the lacy, slightly bronzy-green foliage makes a low mound. Neither the single nor the double kind grows more than six inches high and neither is difficult to grow in good, well-drained soil in sun or partial shade. These adonis (there is also *A. vernalis* which flowers in April and May) should not, in fairness, be faulted for deciding to retire into dormancy during June. The somewhat bare patches they leave can be sown with some dwarf inoffensive annual to give colour for the rest of the summer without seriously harming the adonis.

February is a much more likely period for the Christmas rose, *Helleborus niger*, to flower than late December. Its white saucers are always appealing, but for me its ranking is below that of the March-flowering helleborus complex which mostly go under the name *Helleborus orientalis*. There are several other not often seen species which are not far removed from what we accept as *orientalis*, but there seems to be little certainty as to which is which. One certainty is that as members of a group if not a genus, they are very promiscuous and interbreed unashamedly. The true *orientalis* is said to be white-flowered, but although white often appears in seed-raised plants, the rest range from deep plum-purple to apple-blossom-pink and ivory-green. All have bowl- or saucer-shaped flowers in which yellowish stamens stand up, but some have the most delicate and intriguing red or purple spots inside the petal bowl.

Over many years several good forms have been selected and increased by division, but they are slow growing and therefore expensive to buy. Not so as a mixture, however, and it is this which ranks as my favourite for March, though flowering continues well into April and begins in February if the winter is mild. The flowers nestle on deep green, much divided foliage which is virtually evergreen, a new crop of leaves coming as flowering fades. It is not only the sheer beauty of their flowers when one looks at them closely which makes them so appealing. Nor is it just because they provide interest so early in the year, and so bravely stand up to belated wintry conditions. They respond to severe frosts by drooping rather dolefully, yet when relative warmth returns they at once perk up unharmed. Their other attribute is that they will grow in places which would be quite inhospitable to most other spring-flowering perennials, in shady places which become quite dry in summer. Mind you, they do best where the soil is good and where their roots can reach downwards and outwards, and it would be a pity to place them where the soil is dry and hungry if a better spot exists. A little mulching will be appreciated, and because the clumps slowly but steadily expand and are best left undisturbed for years, they should not be planted less than eighteen inches apart in a group. Seedlings may occur and it is these that are most often offered for sale, for they get away more readily than divisions of old plants.

The greater the range of plants flowering in a given month or period, the more difficult it will be for me to mention just one as favourite. There is more to it than sheer display, which might tempt one to make a choice according to one's favourite colour. As a boy the sight of marsh marigold (known as kingcup in the Fens) used to give me a rare thrill. It still does, but as *Caltha palustris* it has no adaptability beyond its preference for moisture and it remains essentially a waterside subject. Not so the double form 'Plena', which I find is a quite reliable perennial so long as it is not allowed to become dry after its bright display in spring. It is semi-prostrate in habit and sends sprays of perfectly double flowers outwards rather than upwards, of the brightest, glistening yellow imaginable. At a time when most other perennials are only just beginning to wake up, *C. palustris* 'Plena' makes a really eye-catching display, given a sunny spot in good soil. The rounded leaves soon follow to make a deep green backcloth, and stay green all summer provided, as remarked, the plants are not allowed to dry out. They can, of course, be grown beside a pool where one exists, but otherwise it is a good idea to sink around them one or more perforated cans which would otherwise be dumped in the dustbin. With their rims at ground level under the leaves they will be unobtrusive and if these are filled every two or three days in dry periods after flowering during summer, the roots will be kept moist. It is a good practice to divide and replant these calthas once every three years, in early autumn.

The pulmonarias or lungworts cannot be left out, and one in particular is my favourite, flowering as it does at the same time as the caltha and having much the same habit. The blue of both *P. angustifolia* 'Azurea' and the slightly later and dwarfer 'Munstead Blue' are in perfect contrast and equally cheering when spring warmth is elusive. They grow quite well in shade which is not bone dry, but, like most plants, respond to good treatment. Indeed, several other reputed shade lovers besides the lungworts do better in open positions where the soil is good, moist or 'strong' than in shade where tree roots and summer drought is a hindrance to good growth. Many other pulmonarias exist, with pink, blue and white flowers, but these two appeal most to me for their earliness, neatness and brilliance. They should be divided and replanted in early autumn.

A lifetime spent among plants in considerable variety is, I find, after all not conducive to picking favourites on a monthly flowering basis. I have to try to feel detached, to discount what certain plants have meant to me in terms of growing and propagating them. The greater the challenge and effort incurred the more it tends to distort the vision and one's estimation of their intrinsic beauty and garden worthiness. In this context the double wake Robin, *Trillium grandiflorum* 'Plenum' ranks very highly indeed, taking into account the care and thought I have given it over many years. The pure white, full-petalled flowers, up to two inches across, are in perfect harmony with the triple-leaved foliage, and, for all their fragile looking purity, the flowers unsullied for a longer time than any other double white flower I know. A pinkish tinge comes as they begin to fade, as it does with the single flowered form, though not so marked as in the western American species *T. ovatum*. *T. grandiflorum* is native to the eastern American woodlands, and beautiful though it is, I prefer the western species as a single and it is earlier to flower. It, too, has a double form which so far has eluded me, dearly as I would love to have it.

Only the single *T. grandiflorum* sets seeds, and though it takes a few years from germination to flowering, the double-flowered form takes years to produce offsets large enough to detach. Leaving any urge to propagate aside, plants can be left alone to form a clump to produce a score or more of flowers given the light, humus-rich soil it prefers. My first stock came from Montreal in 1957 with the advice that heavy soil suited it best, and this I gave to the nine original crowns. But although they made new fibrous roots and flowered quite well when about nine inches high, it took five years to treble the stock by simple division. It took fifteen years more to have sufficient reserves to allow a few to go to buyers avid for it. And although a slightly quicker method of increase has been found by trial and error, it still takes five years and a surgical operation on a fat crown for the resultant offspring to reach flowering size by careful nursing and nurturing. Over the years the soil used has become lighter until eventually the best response came when it was planted in a peat bed which contains only 60 per cent peat, the rest being in a mixture of bark, loam and sharp sand in more or less equal proportions. Growth is best in dappled shade, and I find a puckish delight in the envious remarks made by American visitors and the slides I am able to show when over there.

Another trillium deserves inclusion. It is the maroon-flowered *T. sessile*, although this colour is sometimes assigned to *T. chloropetalum* which I, cussedly perhaps, refuse to do by leaving the latter name for the pale greenish-yellow trillium. Growth of both is similar. Both, too, have handsome triple-lobed, marble blotched leaves. The three petals of *T. sessile* stand up boldly above the leafy collar and hold their colour for a long time – for three to four weeks in April and May. It is about eighteen inches tall. Its roots grow deeply into the rich soil it prefers, but it is a more vigorous plant than *T. grandiflorum* as well as being taller. Although not difficult to raise from seed, the seedlings need to be left in the row for two years, and two years more after transplanting will bring some up to flowering size. A seven-year-old plant is quite spectacular.

It is natural that spring-flowering plants are much less tall than those which are subjected to a longer period of warmth before they open up their blooms. There is a whole range of tiny alpines for March, April and May, and one of these which has always appealed to me is *Asperula suberosa*. Also known as *A. arcadiensis* it is arcadian in its miniature perfection, having a profusion of tiny tubular flowers of clear light pink borne above slender, woolly grey stems. The tiny grey leaves are soft to the touch and form a low mound no more than two inches high. For me it has been a charmer ever since I bought my first four plants for stock way back in 1926, and it also was the first choice alpine to be propagated by me for sale. Although hardy enough, a very gritty soil, preferably not acid, is essential, and as it is entirely fibrous rooted it responds to careful division.

Another favourite with many, many other admirers must be included here. It is *Dicentra spectabilis*. The name Bleeding Heart cannot be applied to the all white form 'Alba', but another folk name can, to both the pink and the white forms. This is Lady in the Bath, but you have to detach one of the dangling locket-shaped flowers and hold it upside down to see that the name is amusingly apt. These are lovely plants to come from very unlovely fleshy roots, but there is delight in watching the way in which the growth develops. It unfurls its deeply cut, rather fragile foliage through which stems, arching a little, expand to carry rows of pendant flowers in a most charming and distinctive fashion. The type is deep pink with a whitish pistil (forming the lady) and the foliage is glaucous. The white variety 'Alba' has much lighter green leaves and the flowers are milky-white. Both are superb plants for good deep soil in a mainly sunny place, sheltered if possible from strong winds, although the plants themselves are fully hardy.

June is the month when perennials fully capture the senses of all who love them. The earliest flowers have played their part and the magic of spring has merged into bountiful summer, which there are still the high summer glories to come with no signs yet of fading to be seen to remind one that autumn is not many weeks away. June is the month when reds and pink show up most, and where heucheras are happy these make a notable contribution, not only in terms of colour but in the graceful way they grow with myriads of little bells dangling from slender stalks above leafy evergreen mounds. Sadly, however, I have to admit that they do not flourish so well at Bressingham as they did in deep, freer draining Oakington soil with its limier content. Their tendency to become woody-crowned calls for mulching to encourage the formation of fibrous roots, as an alternative to deeper replanting every three or four years in enriched soil, adding sand and lime where needed. My father first grew them about 1912 having seen their cut-flower potential. The smaller-flowered, taller *brizoides* type proved more suitable than the shorter, brighter *sanguinea*, with larger bells, and a batch of seedlings he selected in the early 1920s held the best of both species. This he increased by division, and, by 1926, when I joined him, he had a few hundreds from which flowers sent to Covent Garden yielded very good returns. In 1928 a plant in flower was sent to one of the Royal Horticultural Society's Westminster show and there it gained an award of merit as *Heuchera brizoides* 'Bloom's Variety'. This, to us, appeared as a tremendous breakthrough, heralding prosperity and progress and an end to hard times which had hampered and plagued us for years. Hundreds of plants were set aside for the expected sales, while the stock for flower cutting was increased to thousands.

But surprisingly there was very little demand for plants after deciding that advertising would not be necessary for something with an A.M., R.H.S. after its name. 'Never mind, the flowers will make some money,' said Father, voicing his own special interest. But Father, unthinkingly, made an error. The Covent Garden commission salesman who had made good prices on our heucheras previously were upset by a letter Father wrote complaining about poor returns on some other flowers sent in advance of the heucharas in the following year, 1929. They saw his complaint, rightly or wrongly, as a slur on their integrity and refused to handle any more of his consignments. No other salesman anywhere was able to make such good prices. A year later my parents took over a Mildenhall glasshouse nursery and left me to raise perennials and alpines for sale.

Such Bressingham varieties of heuchera as 'Red Spangles', 'Scintillation', 'Coral Cloud' (an improvement on 'Bloom's Variety'), 'Pretty Polly' and 'Freedom' are still my favourites. Two more recent ones originating from the species *cylindrica* are named 'Green Ivory' and 'Greenfinch'. These grow strongly and flower freely and are much in demand by flower arrangers. And the name Bressingham Hybrids is seen in many catalogues as seed or seedlings to give a mixture which includes a wide range of colour. Heucheras need above all good drainage, and, apart from having pretty evergreen foliage, they can be replanted whenever conditions are suitable, but old woody root growth should be cut away and discarded. A cross, as a result of Percy Piper's 'fiddling' between a heuchera and a tiarella resulted in *Heucherella* 'Bridget Bloom', named after my eldest daughter. It has more open pink flowers borne in fifteen-inch sprays and is a gem, flowering not only in June but often again later above pretty golden-green foliage. Of course, it's a favourite of mine but it needs to be grown in light but rich soil with a low lime content, and in part shade for preference.

I cannot leave June without mention of a blue herbaceous clematis. *Clematis integrifolia* grows about eighteen inches tall and has Oxford blue flowers with turned-back petals. But that is not all, for the flowers are followed by fluffy seed heads which are quite an attraction on their own. The stems are inclined to flop, but at such a modest height this is no disability, though, if supported by peasticks, they are apt to grow taller. The plants are long lived, making sizeable clumps in any decent soil in sun. A form named 'Hendersoni' is a little larger flowered. Anyone keen on planning for colour might do well to use it with heucheras but not in front of them. It would be better to use a blue campanula in front. I am very partial to the campanula hybrids 'Stella' and the deeper blue 'Constellation'. Both carry myriads of open starry flowers in sprays for a long time and often give a second crop if cut back after the first flowering. Another first-rate species is *C. muralis* which I obstinately refuse to call *portenschlagiana*, now said to be correct. This species has lavender-blue flowers on six-inch stems; it is more upright than 'Stella', and flowers on and off all summer.

The best of the *muralis* hybrids was raised by my old friend Will Ingwersen as a cross between *portenschlagiana* and the rampant *porscharskyana*. Rather than follow the oft-used practice of combining parental names (in this case to coin a possible name of 'portenschars-kyana'), Will wisely decided to name it Birch Hybrid.

So that is two blue flowers and it has to be two pinks also, both fairly dwarf and both flowering over a longer period than the month of June itself. The *Centaurea hypoleuca* I grow is different to the one I saw under that name in Kew Gardens, but having grown it unchallenged for nearly fifty years I am sticking to it. It is a very good plant with silvery-grey leaves in mound formation and cornflower-type blossoms of soft pink. The stems are wiry, arching a little to give an overall height of about fifteen inches. The other pink is *Diascia elegans*, a relatively recent introduction from South Africa. There were others, one being a two-foot tall charmer named *D. rigescens* with an amazing succession of pink-lipped flowers. I went a bundle on it in 1983 and produced a large stock, only to find that it failed to survive the hard frosts of the two winters following. But *elegans*, which came to me in time to test it in the near zero temperatures of January, 1985, came through unscathed. Its habit is more mat forming than that of *D. rigescens*, and, as such, quite vigorous and easily divided. The sprays of soft pink flowers are about fifteen inches tall, and all it seems to need to give a good long display is not too heavy soil, and sun.

There is little need to apologise for including several plants I have named and introduced. They would scarcely have been selected as worthy plants in the first place had they not appealed to me, and one which has become widely popular at home and abroad is *Achillea*

'Moonshine'. Yet it was only by lucky chance that the original plant was not thrown away. Percy Piper raised a score or so of seedlings from a hybrid achillea from Switzerland which, though quite pretty, struck me as being a weakling. So, too, were most of the seedlings, but with more hope than excitement I staked two of the best, giving them the provisional names 'Sunshine' and 'Moonshine.' Both rotted away during the following winter. The row of plants ended in the shade of an old apple tree and although none of the others were saved, the one nearest the tree was left because of its silvery-grey foliage and it was the only one which had not flowered. It stayed there for three years and still failed to flower, but a spring came with a group space in the garden needing a fill-gap so I divided the clump and planted the pieces with no thought of it flowering. But it did flower in this sunny, stoney spot and its eighteen-inch high lemon-yellow heads were so attractive above the foliage that it had to take the name 'Moonshine'. But for that vacant space it could well have been dumped because the apple tree was dying and due to come out.

It is not only the ability to give a colourful display which counts when reflecting on one's favourite plants, and certainly not the size of the flower. Sometimes quite small flowers lacking in brilliance have an overall grace and charm. Two such plants come to mind for June. One is *Amsonia salicifolia* which carries the specific synonym of *tabernae-montana* and, as always, I go for the lesser number of syllables where a choice exists. At first glance it seems an unlikely member of the periwinkle (*Vinca*) family, for it is a truly herbaceous clump-forming perennial. *Salicifolia* means willow-leaved and both leaves and stems are indeed willowy, arching a little from the base to about three feet. Near the tip come small clusters of tiny, light blue, somewhat tubular flowers which make a display for several weeks. Fading is scarcely noticed for the shapely greenery stays on until autumn.

The second small-flowered choice, *Gillenia trifoliata*, is of very similar habit. But this is a member of the rose family and serrated, narrow leaves clothe the strong, wiry stems. There is a hint of golden-green in its overall appearance, and the white flowers stand out despite their smallness, remaining attractive for five or six weeks in the dampish soil it prefers, with some high or dappled shade. The richer the soil the better it will perform, but heavy, poorly-drained soil will be resented – unlike the amsonia which is much more adaptable. Gillenia roots are tough and both it and the amsonia can be left for several years to form large clumps.

Both paeonies and irises have been omitted simply because their beauty is so fleeting. I believe that over one thousand varieties of the June-flowering germanica type iris have been registered by the Americans, but there is one American native species which I like very much. It is *I. missouriensis*, growing no more than two feet tall with a wealth of light blue flowers of satiny texture and quite trouble free. If I had to throw out all other irises for some reason, this is the one I would keep, bar one, to be mentioned when winter comes.

July is the peak month for colour among perennials and so it is all the more difficult to pick out just one or two favourites. To do so colour-wise may be easier. The blue will have to be a scabiosa, not the well-known and well-loved, taller *caucasica* varieties, but a dwarf species named *graminifolia* which suffers from undeserved neglect. The pin-cushion flowers an inch or two across come in silvery-grey tufts or tuffets of narrow leaves up to eight inches above ground. The stems have a maximum height of less than twelve inches and keep coming week after week until early autumn. There is also a pink form which appeared at Bressingham under the name 'Pink Cushion'. All they need is well-drained soil and sun. Both blue and white occur in an aconitum we named 'Blue Sceptre'. As a bicolour it stands out well and in good contrast with the shiny, deep green leaves below. It is the dwarfest aconitum cultivar I know at two and a half feet and is stiffly erect with the flower spikes having secondaries as the centre one fades.

CHAPTER ELEVEN

More Favourites

The first purchase of plants I ever made was of a hundred seedlings in twenty kinds for five shillings. I had just left school with the conviction that what they were trying to teach me was of far less value than what I could learn by working with plants.

During the year that I worked with my father I sent out of my savings ten shillings to Prichard's of Christchurch, specialists in perennial plants, for which they sent me twelve different herbaceous potentillas. It was a genus which appealed to me as a whole from reading about them, and those I coveted most were the herbaceous hybrids. At the time I was inclined to be a bookish Francophile and such names as 'Arc in Ciel', 'Flambeau', 'Mons. Rouillard' and 'Gloire de Nancy' were an added attraction, especially when I learned that they had been introduced a long time ago. That was in 1923 and I have kept a few of that original set ever since.

A further appeal was the suffusing colours on the same flower, such as the rich mahogany-red and orange in 'Gloire de Nancy' and the lighter, brighter combination in 'Wm. Rollison'. 'Yellow Queen' is a silvery-leaved semi-double, self-coloured variety, but the suffusion occurs with slight variations in several more which are now no longer in circulation. All these have leaves which show their relationship with strawberries, and hybrids still occur, including my own named 'Blazeaway', in which red and orange make a bright display. 'Flamenco' is a very bright single red which occurred at Bressingham as a self-sown seedling, and, at close on two feet tall, it is taller than most. The most popular is the so-called 'Gibson's Scarlet', also single and bright red. Its name is suspect because I once learned on good authority that it was raised by a Cornishman, one Captain Pinwillis, and that George Gibson, whom I knew as a somewhat thrusting nurseryman, gave it his own name which has stuck. Incidentally, a first-class Dutch plantsman, Willy van Egmond, once persuaded me to buy *Potentilla* 'Congo' – not that I needed much persuading being a sucker for the herbaceous kinds of which I have over sixty. But after growing 'Congo' for several years, found there was no difference between this and 'Gibson's Scarlet', making its origins even more obscure.

Colour suffusion is also to be seen in several of the heleniums in which bronze, brown, yellow and orange play their part. Although they may rank as indispensible border plants they can be faulted on two counts. One is their top-heaviness which calls for supports to be provided in some rich soils, the other that where the soil is poor or dry, their stem leaves fade before flowering is over, so spoiling the overall effect. Some varieties still in commerce are much too tall, especially when grown in narrow, one-sided beds. Percy Piper's seedling which we named 'Coppelia' has streaked orange and brown flowers and is not too tall at three and a half feet, but I find our other two, 'Bruno' and 'Butterpat', prone to flop in a damp season. Both are later than 'Coppelia', but my favourite is the dwarf 'Wyndley' at only two feet tall. Its origin has eluded me and all attempts to raise variations on its deep orange-steaked flowers have failed – as with the inaptly named mahogany-brown-flowered 'Crimson Beauty', which is even dwarfier. Both these dwarf varieties have been in cultivation for well over fifty years. A score or so new varieties have been raised in Europe since then yet all have been much taller despite the advantage of dwarfness. It points to some genetic quirk which, so far, is beyond the ability of hybridists to overcome.

Heleniums are best divided and replanted in enriched soil about every three years, but it can be longer in the case of both helianthus and heliopsis. The 'Hel' comes from the Greek word for the sun, *helios*, and all have some kinship with what we know as sunflowers (forms of the annual *Helianthus annuus*). Of the perennial helianthus by far the best are the varieties of *H. decapetalus*. They include the well-known 'Loddon Gold' a double-flowered yellow variety, bush-forming to a height of about five feet, 'Morning Sun', rich yellow, and Capernoch

Star, semi-double. Most other species are weedy and do not deserve the ever-increasing space they take up.

Heliopsis are not like that. They form expanding clumps but are never invasive and flower for a long time at modest heights of three to four feet. All are yellow, some single, some, like 'Golden Plume', almost double, and, being heavier, more likely to need supporting. I like them because they are not troublesome, do not need frequent replanting and flower for a very long time. But there are far too many varieties. That eminent German plantsman, Karl Foerster, raised and named about a dozen before he died at the ripe old age of ninety-five a few years ago. They vary very little and the best I know is 'Desert King', but there is still a demand for 'Goldgreenheart' whose semi-double flowers have a greenish tinge.

If there were only a few hemerocallises and hostas in existence I would be strongly inclined to bring them in as favourites. But much as I admire them and rank them as being indispensible, there is now such a bewildering welter of cultivars that to mention even a modest selection would be inadequate. As with irises and paeonies we can thank – or maybe blame – the American enthusiasts for raising, naming and registering far more than would be wise for any nurseryman to offer. I believe that the hemerocallis – which they prefer to call day lilies – run to well over a thousand varieties, and any nurseryman who attempted to keep abreast of the annual turnout to offer them to his customers would soon go bankrupt or crazy. And now the hosta craze is gathering momentum. I have no figures but would say that the number of registered cultivars has well passed two hundred and fifty. Some have quite fanciful names and a few are positively absurd such as 'Oompa'.

My son Adrian, despite some misgivings on my part, decided we should hold trials of hemerocallis and hostas in order to pick out for propagation and subsequent sales a reasonable range of the best or most distinctive. My misgivings were, and still are, on the grounds that by the time a selection is made from the one hundred and fifty or so varieties on trial, as many more will have emerged from the hybridisers. We shall see, but rather cussedly I am going to pick out as favourites just one of each genus which appeals to me. The hemerocallis chosen is a dwarf one named 'Stella d'Oro'. At fifteen to eighteen inches tall it integrates well as a frontal group to give good foliage and a long season of rich golden-yellow colour. Such a subject is needed among low-growing plants along the front of a bed or border to break up the uniformity with something erect and of good overall appearance. The hosta is one which I have grown for forty years and it is, by contrast, the tallest of its kind in flower, some four and a half feet. It is *Hosta rectifolia*, also known as 'Tallboy'. What makes it outstanding in my view is that it maintains its display far longer than any other hosta I know. It has lavender-blue flowers and the stately spikes are enhanced by stem leaves. It needs no fussing, grows in full sun or shade and can be relied upon, except where bone dry, to give a long display year after year. Such a performance has ruled out any necessity to put it in Adrian's trials.

Omitting also irises, paeonies and oriental poppies from my list of favourites does not mean that I dislike them or fail to appreciate their fulsome, gorgeous beauty. They are not included for reasons already touched on: that there are too many varieties from which to make a selection of just one or two and that they have such a short season in flower. Conversely, I am inclined to mention plants which are not so spectacular but do flower for a long time and this, to my mind, is an essential consideration so far as merit is concerned.

The polygonums as a genus are not widely grown partly, I suspect, because a few are decidedly invasive. But I have three favourites which are by way of being choice, because they make anything but rapid spread and have a somewhat narrow range of adaptability. This merely means, however, that they like reasonably rich, light soil which does not quickly dry out, but it does not mean that they like it boggy.

Curiously, though, a visitor once told me that he had seen *Polygonum milettii*, one of my three, growing in shallow water in Nepal. Mine were doing fine in rich, light loam, but the information prompted me to plant a few in the bed of a trickling stream where, after a year or two, they died without making anything of a show of their intensely red poker-like flowers. These pokers are little more than a foot tall above lots of dark green, narrow leaves, and they come on and off for much of the summer. *P. macrophyllum* has arching, wavy, strap-like leaves with the same clumpy habit. The pokers are clear pink about eighteen inches tall and with this as with *milettii* one sees that other feature which makes for overall charm, foliage which is fully complementary to the flowers. My third polygonum is different, for the knotty stems of *P. sphaerostachyum* come in such profusion that one sees little of the base. These stems are branched, tipped by little pokers of bright deep pink. Flowering begins in late spring and will continue until well into September if the plants are trimmed back in July.

A fourth species also comes to mind. *P. campanulatum* is later flowering with heads of tiny shell-pink flowers topping dense, leafy, bush-like growth from July until the autumn frosts cut it back to ground level. The vigorous roots are not deep or invasive, being surface feeding and easily checked. This is an excellent, undeservedly neglected plant for those who have a dampish place in sun or part shade, on a slope or on the level.

Another polygonum, *P. amphibium*, merely intrigues me as a wildling. It ranked as a weed which ran around but never flowered where I decided to make a two acre lake in 1955 (see Chapter Three, More Ups and Downs). We took out two to three feet of soil and subsoil, believing that this would be the end to a large patch of this knotweed. But not so, for a year after the water came in the polygonum came up to rest its spear-shaped leaves on the surface, and thereafter it has regularly flowered, pink and pretty.

Most astilbes have both foliage and flowers in perfect harmony, but not many last long enough in flower for me to be greatly impressed by this, despite their sumptuousness where happy in moist soil. They also prefer some shade, but, in my experience, lack of shade provision for astilbes is mitigated by well-fed and moistened soil, while lack of moisture is to some extent offset by some shade. The height range of astilbes is about six inches to six feet, but my favourite is 'Sprite', barely one foot high. It is chosen not only because I selected and named it from a batch of Percy Piper's seedlings, but because it flowers for such a long time and is more adaptable than most. The dark, deeply incised leaves make a perfect foil for the sprays of tiny flowers which although not quite white do not have in them more than a tinge of pink. At any rate 'Sprite' is both colourful and attractive enough for the supply to be never enough to meet the demand.

As July merges into August and yellows tend to dominate gardens, phlox and agapanthus are now a compensating feature and the crocosmias are coming into their pride. Some pride for Percy and myself because his fiddling with crocosmia yielded some outstanding hybrids when I suggested crossing two species for colour and reliability. There are five genera all mixed up here to make matters very confusing, prompting me arbitrarily to lump *Curtonus*, *Montbretia*, *Antholyza* and *Tritonia* all under the name *Crocosmia* for the sake of simplicity. *Crocosmia masonorum* was reputed to be not fully hardy until the winter of 1963 penetrated below corm level for several weeks and left them unharmed. So was *Antholyza paniculata*, and the first cross was between these two. It resulted in a much larger brighter flowered seedling, now named 'Lucifer', with masses of sword-like leaves and four-foot sprays of fiery red flowers. From one corm has come thousands of plants now in gardens in this country and abroad.

'Firebird' is an improvement on the other parent, *Crocosmia masonorum*, which has its flowers upfacing on arching, wiry stems. This feature makes for constant appeal with the orange-red so warm and striking. This is a three-footer but the deep burnt-orange 'Emberglow' is barely two feet tall, while 'Spitfire' and 'Bressingham Blaze' fall in between these heights. Between them from 'Lucifer', the earliest to flower, to 'Emberglow' they give a six-week period of colour. Two more make their debut in 1987: the flame-coloured 'Bressingham Beacon' and the soft light orange 'Jenny Bloom'.

Phlox must be passed over for the same reason as irises and paeonies, namely there are too many of them to make a single or very limited choice, although they are needed to tone down the predominant yellow shades of high summer. There is another plant of the latter colour which ranks highly, the well-known *Rudbeckia* 'Goldsturm', best by far of the black-eyed susans. In reasonably good not too dry soil, I have known it to flower from June until late October, its rayed yellow flowers contrasting so well with the black cone on two-and-a-half-foot stems, and it will, unlike most other rudbeckias, take some shade. The purple coneflower, listed sometimes as *Rudbeckia* and sometimes under *Echinacea*, often has the fault of drooping petals of a rather dull rosy-purple. We spent years trying to breed out this fault, especially noticeable in the then best-known variety 'The King'. When finally success came I named the new varieties 'Robert Bloom', this having broader horizontal petals of a warm rosy-salmon shade and stiffly upright three-foot stems.

Aster frikartii makes an excellent companion for all the August-flowering perennials already described. Its light lavender-blue daisy-type flowers with yellow centres on much branched stems are a joy for many weeks. Herr Frikart of Stäfa near Zurich raised three others, named 'Eiger', 'Jungfrau' and 'Mönch', after the three famous peaks in the Bernese Oberland. They do not vary greatly from his original, which also carries the name 'Wunda von Stäfa', but whichever one has or obtains it will be valued highly. The cross Herr Frikart made was between an *Aster amellus* and *A. thompsonii*. The latter is now rare, but not so its charming dwarf form 'Nanus' and this is a firm favourite for me. It makes a shapely little grey-leaved bush about fifteen inches high studded with one-inch, starry-blue, yellow-centred flowers for weeks on end. It is slow to expand into a neat clump, best in light soil and sun, and if, after a time, it seems to be pushing itself a little out of the soil give it a mulch of a sandy mixture or replant in spring.

With August some of the kniphofias will have finished flowering, but 'Little Maid' is showing its creamy buds and will soon give her long display of ivory-yellow. The credit for this charmer goes to Beth Chatto, and my only involvement was to persuade her to change the name slightly from 'Small' to 'Little'. This she did with good grace, knowing, as we both did, that it was by way of a petite version of 'Maid of Orleans', which has become very scarce. So have several of the older varieties due to a virus made more prevalent, I fancy, by over-propagation – as with the named Russell lupins. Now I use only two- or three-year-old clumps for dividing, and apply dustings or waterings of the fungicide Benlate, which seems to have overcome the trouble.

We lost almost the entire stock of some outstanding offspring of the late-flowering, dwarf and grassy-leaved *K. galpinii*, and of those only 'Bressingham Comet' and 'Gleam' are on the way back – I hope. Kniphofias, which, incidentally, are so varied in their flowering times as to cover all the summer months from May to October, cannot bear poor drainage. Nor are they 100 per cent hardy, especially when damp soil freezes solid. We use straw to protect the most susceptible kinds, but I have found them to survive when the roots of trees are not too far away to keep the soil more open in winter.

Kniphofias almost invariably show up at a distance like sentinels, especially the taller ones, and should not be hemmed in with other plants to spoil their stateliness. But the tricyrtises require close scrutiny to be fully aware of their distinctive beauty. These members of the lily family have no bright colours, but the leafy stems of *Tricyrtis formosana* and *T. stolonifera* have some open-petalled flowers in a lilac shade prettily spotted with crimson. *T. formosana* is my favourite because it grows erectly, keeps to a neat clump, flowers for several weeks and grows in any reasonable soil or sun or partial shade. No more than this can be asked of any plant.

An entirely different looking member of the *Liliaceae* is opening out in August, but will remain colourful until late October. *Liriope muscari* (now said to be correctly *L. macrophylla*) is as adaptable if not more so than the *Tricyrtis*. The foliage is tufty, broadly grassy and evergreen, rising nine inches or so above ground. The wiry, erect stems carry pokers of tiny lavender-lilac beads standing a few inches above the tuft. Once open they stay with barely noticeable fading until November, and, because it will grow in any but the heaviest marly soil, in sun or shade, it ranks very highly indeed. Yet it is only just becoming noticed for the excellent plant it is. I only wish the variegated leaved forms would grow as well in England as they do in America, but, sadly, they resent our damp winters and lack the summer heat to give them strength. All are drought resistant and store up reserves in small tubers among the otherwise fibrous roots. As a genus – not a large one – they will stay happily for years without having to divide and replant, making tight clumps a foot or more in diameter.

September has been partially covered already simply because several of my August choices carry on until then. A deciduous grass which contrasts well with liriope – and much else where dwarfish plants are grown – is *Hakonechloa macra aurea variegata*. It is a pity that it has such a mouthful of a name, but it is well worth a place given good light soil and sun. The bright golden streaked blades, six to eight inches long, are dense, rising from a tough and wiry rootstock which is not invasive. Although it will spread, one cannot but be glad to see it flourishing for it is very bright indeed and can be forgiven for not being evergreen and for having insignificant flowers.

Calamintha nepetoides is not often seen but it is such a cheerful, adaptable little plant for late flowering. It has a somewhat bushy habit and a height of about twenty inches, small light green leaves and a profusion of pale blue flowers which last for a long time. It does not mind some shade, looks very well on a wall and will stay put giving no trouble for years, from a slowly expanding mat-like rootstock. It is the kind of plant that some writers describe as having a quiet beauty of its own. It blends well with a plant that I consider to be well up in the top ten introductions since World War II, namely *Sedum* 'Autumn Joy'. The German nursery on which it was raised suffered the effects of several British bombs. When I visited Ronsdorf not long afterwards, Georg Arends explained how difficult it had been to keep going so close to the much bombed Ruhr. But he held no bitterness against the British and asked me if I would introduce the sedum (then under its German name 'Herbstfreude') along with two or three other of his hybrids. Naturally I was more than happy to do this. The succulent, glaucous leaves on thick stems indicate a promise, but when the wide flat heads reveal myriads of small salmon-pink flowers in September, that promise is more than fulfilled. And, as the longer nights arrive so a russety hue takes over before finally the long display comes to an end. It is a little taller and more robust than its 'ice plant' parent, *S. spectabile*, and has achieved such widespread popularity that I cannot imagine many discerning gardeners not having it in their gardens already.

Not many tall-growing plants have been mentioned, but there are two that must be. *Artemisia lactiflora* is the only member of its genus I know worth growing for its flowers, and, unlike most artemias, the foliage is green not grey. Also unlike the rest it does best in good soil, not too dry, and the leafy stems rise stiffly to a good four feet to be topped by a fine plume of creamy-white, congested florets – very striking when viewed against a dark background.

The cimicifugas (the name means bugbane) are also white but much more slender in growth with just the form and grace to offset the dominance of michaelmas daisies and chrysanthemums. There are some that flower in July and August, but *C. simplex* 'White Pearl' and 'Elstead' are superb for September and October, with ivory-white pokers up to six feet tall when grown in the rich soil they prefer – neither too wet nor very dry. Given this they will take to sun or shade and never need supports for their strong, graceful stems, which rise early and are attractive in leaf long before flowering begins. Purplish-leaved forms have emerged from the tall *ramosa* species which flowers a month or so earlier. Both *C. ramosa* 'Brunette' and 'Atropurpurea' are sure to be in strong demand.

The rounded, indented leaves of *Saxifraga fortunei* are attractive all summer, making a mound only six inches or so high. The species has green foliage with the undersides a little bronzy, but the so-called 'Wada's Form' and *rubrifolia* are much more colourful, in shades of almost beetroot and bronze-red respectively, with the undersides even brighter. One wonders (if lacking in faith) whether they are meant to flower, but, come October, they suddenly erupt into nine- to ten-inch sheaves of starry white as if by magic. These are plants for cool shade, a term which, in practice, means good soil which does not dry out and shade not too dense and overhanging. A mainly north-facing wall suits them well, and although spring frosts may spoil the first tender shoots they will recover. Although I take the precaution of protecting them over winter with oak leaves, some folk tell me that they are hardy enough without it. They do, however, respond to a little mulch in spring, having no deep roots, as an alternative to replanting every two or three years.

November brings out the pink trumpets of *Nerine bowdeni* and the dainty *schizostylis*, Kaffir lilies, with flowers in pink, red, salmon and, at last, white. Nerines like to be left alone but not the Kaffir lilies which spread quickly in the rich, sandy soil they like, but which need winter protection and frequent replanting. Almost anything that flowers in dull November is of special value and worth caring for, but if these two may linger on into the dampness of dismal December, then the variegated evergreen perennials come into their own to brighten up the worst of winter.

For many years I doubted if what I grew as *Carex morrowii* 'Variegata' was the true plant. It formed quite large clumps with bladed, deep green leaves having a buff-yellow midriff. As a check I asked Kew Gardens to send a plant of the true, all-green *C. morrowii*, but what they sent was one much more variegated, which struck me as being much more attractive. From that one piece a large stock was built up over the years by annual division, and when I was asked to give it a cultivar name to go with an export order to New Zealand, it became 'Evergold', even if it was more yellow than gold and any green present is scarcely noticeable.

Recently a really golden form of the grassy-leaved *Acorus gramineus* named 'Ogon' has arrived to become as much, if not more, of a favourite. Its origin is obscure but my plants come as a result of Adrian's peregrinations abroad and it's up to me to increase it just as fast as I can. It is only six inches high and is so far an easy grower in any sunny place, as is *Carex* 'Evergold'. Neither of these plants bears flowers and somehow one feels that if they did they would be superfluous and detract from the effect.

The showiest of all evergreen variegated perennials must surely be *Iris foetidissima* 'Variegata' – not because it is brighter in leaf than the foregoing, so much as because it has longer, broader leaves. These are twelve to fifteen inches long and nearly two inches broad, each leaf being striped vertically, half primrose-yellow and half pea-green. It is, moreover, very adaptable to shade and though not tuberous rooted does not mind it being dry in competition with tree roots. Naturally, it grows more lustily in fairly good soil, and whether in sun or shade will steadily expand. The species is the Gladwyn or stinking iris which naturalises, but the latter name is rather a disability for it is only the flowers which have a faint and not unpleasant aroma. Not that the purplish-lilac flowers are very significant, and in the variegated form they are quite sparse. Nor do they set seed as does the green-leaved type, to form pods which in autumn open to reveal bright orange-red seeds like little berries.

Here the year's selection has to end. And if I were to begin all over again, I would probably find fifty more favourites, some rare, some well known and loved. If I were able to roam abroad to other gardens, whether botanic, public or private, I am pretty sure there would be some plants to bring back, try out and come to love. The number of perennials of potential garden merit seems to be infinite and it is well beyond the capacity of any one person to know, let alone grow, them all.

CHAPTER TWELVE

Worm's Eye View

There appears to be a considerable gulf between the two main groups of people who are interested in plants. This gulf is not so much between those who garden for pleasure and relaxation and those who grow them for a living, as between these two groups combined and the professional researchers, botanists and taxonomists. The last mentioned are relatively few in number, but what they do and what they dictate so far as nomenclature is concerned affects the rest of us as does the work of researchers into pests and diseases of plants. My use here of the word plants includes hardwood and softwood subjects, trees and weeds. A true botanist makes little distinction between these categories and the taxonomists have botanic names which they use for all and every one of the half million or so different species of plants which inhabit the earth. There is a complicated system of classification and identification and it has to work so that it is internationally used and understood.

The gulf referred to above arises through the academics' apparent disregard for the interests of practical gardeners. Conversely, the latter often fail to appreciate the value of the work and purpose of those professionals, who, it is sometimes suggested, live in ivory towers. It is likely that they become just as excited over a newly discovered plant which could be nothing but an obnoxious weed in the garden as by some exotic or attractive find of immense garden value. A botanist who is also a gardener would take a more appreciative view, but there are some, whose life is based largely on a herbarium where all is lifeless, who might be at a loss to recognise a flowering plant in the garden. Such a botanist could, however, point out and name every part of a plant, describing accurately the type of leaf, stem, root and sexual parts of the flower – which is more than I could do, and this difference I must respect even if what I would call its seed he would refer to as its fruit.

I must also admit that because the botanists home milieu and mine are far apart there is no active conflict. But the taxonomists whose background is botany have a harmless adversary in me for refusing to accept and use what I consider unjustified changes of name which they declare to be correct, completely disregarding common usage. The rule is that the earliest recorded name given to a plant species must take priority. This means in effect that if a plant has been known under one name for no matter how long it becomes invalid if some researcher discovers that an earlier botanist or taxonomist recorded it under another name. With botanic names something of a hindrance to a large number of gardeners already, a name changing just for this reason adds to their difficulty. In my view and that of many others, common usage should take priority over the semantic and not the other way round. Not that there are penalties for sticking to a well-known name, but there can be no realistic or practical justification for adhering to what is merely an imposed rule of academic value only.

Other name changing comes about in the case of genera. It may well be that researchers discover some slight differences between some member species of a genus sufficient to justify it being given, in their view, an entirely new name. But when it comes to changing *Avena* to *Helictotrichon* and *Orchis* to *Dactylorrhiza* I feel compelled to jib and am in favour, obstinately, of keeping the older, much easier name. Not that one could justifiably object to some expert trying to bring order into a given genera's nomenclature if this is in a mess botanically, as many still are. But it only adds to confusion when two such experts independently make changes and amendments which each consider to be necessary and correct, but the conclusions differ, as has happened in the case of hostas. There is no supreme authority to adjudicate on such results.

There has been a spate of researchings and dictums on plant names over the past 50 years. A few nurserymen have attempted to make their catalogue entries conform with the results produced but not always publicised widely. But these catalogues or manuals become very difficult to follow with a plethora of alternative synonyms and cross references – enough to put off a would-be plant purchaser or to make anyone just becoming interested in plants and trying to master botanic names give up in disgust. It is surely asking too much for most of us ordinary folk to go along with changes which after all are to millions of amateur or professional gardeners a disability. It is hard enough for them to assimilate botanical names at the best of times but to discover that *Campanula muralis* should correctly be called *Campanula portenschlagiana* is too much to expect. It is of importance only to the relative few who often are far removed from the realms of practical gardening.

Most of the curatorial staff of botanic gardens are, of course, exempt from this criticism. They are usually practical, knowledgeable people with a keen interest in the intrinsic or decorative value of plants. One cannot but feel sorry for their burden of changing, confusing nomenclature for they can do no other than comply with the edicts which are handed down. Curators have, in general, fewer academic qualifications than the botanists and taxonomists. They have more practical skills and experience and may well feel that they are between two stools. As plantsmen they have to struggle with the problems of nomenclature, and often it is through them changed names have to filter through to both amateur and professional gardeners. A few of the latter, with the gift of easy assimilation, may take to new names with one-upmanship in mind but the majority view them with dismay and distaste.

So much for scientific or botanical names. Let us turn from the botanists and taxonomists to the plant pathologists whose work is vastly different, for the study of plant diseases is closely akin to medical research. They are a relatively small band and not generously funded, and some cures and controls they have effected have had greatly beneficial effects. But so much remains to be discovered with new problems cropping up constantly, with higher priorities pushing aside attention to plants which have only decorative value. Those of us who encounter diseases in the plants we produce for a living appreciate this, but it is disheartening when time after time a negative answer comes as a result of a request for help. We send in material for laboratory inspection in the hope that some disease will be diagnosed and a cure prescribed, only to be told, more often than not, that the only course of action is to burn all the infected plants. But there, what else could they say if they have not the means to tackle more than a few disease problems?

It could be a kind of rebellion against the use of botanical names which causes some people to stick to common or folk names wherever possible. To do so completely would be impossible, especially where there are many species belonging to the same genus, as well as hybrids. There may be no valid objection to such names as hollyhock, lilac, wallflower and pansy being used as a regular thing because everybody knows them. Most gardeners also know that Christmas and Lenten roses, rose of Sharon, rock and sun roses are not roses at all, but the less knowledgeable could well be confused. If one were to try to distinguish between, say, the different species of campanula in cultivation by attaching some folky epithet to bellflower or harebell, then far greater confusion would ensue than by using a botanic name for each of the species.

The Americans are especially prone to use common names. Some nursery catalogues and even books give them priority over the botanical names, in the belief, no doubt, that people will take more readily to them. I have seen garden centres over there where plants carry a label inscribed merely with a common name when it could have been any one of a score or more kinds of its unnamed genus. Such a practice is playing down to ignorance which is as culpable as unjustified name changing by the taxonomists. All who are the least bit interested in gardening should be encouraged to use the regular or best-known botanical name and it is those who break through little by little to find such names acceptable and helpful who are likely to get the greatest pleasure from gardening.

Common usage is of paramount importance and some quite long names having no folk alternative have become a universally accepted part of the gardening vocabulary. No one cavils at rhododendron, chrysanthemum, poinsettia or aspidistra. These became common as names probably because there were no alternatives, but there is every reason why professionals should encourage amateurs to widen their knowledge of botanical names, especially as some plants have more than one common name – often of local origin. So often a common name is applied to a whole genus whereas it properly applies to only one species of that genus. For example 'stonecrop' applies only to *Sedum acre*, which will survive on rocks almost devoid of soil, and which scarcely any other of the very numerous sedums will do. I may be accused of pedantry for making such observations, but there is a need to take a realistic attitude to plant names for the sake of simplicity and a more widely accepted order and method of identification.

This applies also to the classification in garden parlance of plants which fall into differing categories. Scientific classification has to be left to the botanists who not only pontificate on correct nomenclature but decide on the natural order or family to which each genus belongs. What to us seems rather unlikely members of the same family makes sense to them – such as currants and astilbes belonging to the saxifraga, or *Saxifragaceae*, family, raspberries to the rose family, or *Rosaceae.* Some gardeners lacking practical experience are at a loss in matters of hardiness, adaptability and usage when deciding to widen the range of plants they grow. What they may need is some definition as to treatment.

'Hardy plants' is a term which might include any subject, herbaceous, alpine, shrubby, dwarf or tall which is capable of surviving winter frosts. For some people it excludes anything classed as a shrub or hardwood subject, but is nonetheless perennially hardy. This section may include, however, alpine or rock garden plants since they are hardy and perennial whether or not they are herbaceous in behaviour. Herbaceous as a group term by itself is often applied to perennials considered too tall for growing on a rock garden. But it is inadequate because it applies strictly to plants which die down to a perennial rootstock and do not retain their foliage over winter. All very confusing for beginners, and revealing again of a need for us to be more precise in the terminology we use.

It would scarcely be helpful for beginners to be told that it is all a matter of adaptability when they have had no experience of what plants are adaptable for a given site, aspect or climate. But this is where interest really begins and there are plenty of books and a few nursery catalogues which, consulted in advance, can be helpful. These are also a good way of becoming more familiar with plant names, and I for one came to learn quite a lot of names and what they stood for well before I saw them in the flesh, simply by poring over books and descriptive catalogues. From such an exercise some ideas and information on plant adaptability are sure to emerge. Meanwhile, some attempts to define different categories of garden plants may be helpful.

'Perennials' is becoming a more widely used collective term for what were formerly called herbaceous or border plants. Both the latter terms are quite inadequate and misleading. Not all perennials are herbaceous and herbaceous borders are no longer the only sites on which to grow them. They can be, and often still are, grown in the borders between, say, a lawn and a boundary – or screen of shrubs and evergreens. So long as there is a plot of any size, shape or position, perennials can be found to fill it effectively. Very few so-called alpine or rock plants need rocks amongst which to grow and many are quite adaptable to grow as dwarf perennials – which is what they are – either by themselves or in front of taller kinds. There is simply no dividing line between them except on the basis of adaptability to a given site.

Some perennials come from high altitudes and can, therefore, be classed as alpines. Nature has made them adapt to harsh or dry conditions, to become tiny, whether or not they remain as evergreen mats, tufts or hummocks. It is these that require fussing, giving them the sharp drainage they need in gritty soil. Some dislike winter wet so much that they need the protection of glass, though they may otherwise be hardy. Others, more adaptable, are best in a raised bed where their special needs can be met, and their beauty seen more closely. And those of a somewhat shrubby nature can be included because they are less adaptable to ordinary garden conditions.

Of course, not all denizens of ivory towers are solely concerned with the botanical aspects of plants and their naming. Garden architects are apt to build up a mystique which lifts them above the ordinary amateur gardener. As in the legal profession, those who use their services are known as clients and not customers to signify their professional superiority. The fact is, however, that very few garden architects, fully qualified though they may be academically, know very much about plants. My experience of them is, I must admit, not very wide and is based largely on plans some have sent as orders to be filled against the selection specified on such plans. So often a narrow range of plants is specified with many repetitions, so that one is bound to assume that these are the limits of the planner's knowledge of suitable material.

Although I believe more knowledge of plants is required now than formerly to qualify as a full member of the Institute of Landscape Architects, a large gap still exists. I also believe anyone can set up as a landscaper without becoming a member or having academic qualifications. And some of these I do know are better plantsmen than those who can put F.I.L.A. after their name. To my mind a person with a comprehensive knowledge of plants gained from practical experience is likely to give most satisfaction to his clients. I must, or course, add that some top architects sensibly sub-contract to a plantsman who will take charge of the selection and planting to fit in with the overall plan.

The steady increase both in the number of garden owners and those who cater for their needs has had inevitably a two-sided effect. It has allowed some charlatans to take advantage of ignorant garden owners as well as raising to some extent the standards of respectable professionals. This applies both to goods and services and includes producers and purveyors of nursery stock. I know of no trade or industry with such varying standards of quality. Prices vary accordingly but usually the lower the price at which plants are offered, the lower the relative value becomes. This has been borne out time and time again even since a trader came to me to buy up job lots of plants fifty years ago. He made a self satisfied remark which stuck in my memory. 'There's a fool born', he said with a smirk, 'every minute, and I'd be a fool not to take his money if he's fool enough to part with it.' This would-be customer wanted plants which he could divide into small pieces to sell at a fraction of what I would charge him. Surplus seedlings or rooted cuttings would do just as well, he added, because, by having large advertisements in the weekend press, orders at his bargain prices brought him profits.

Such cheap-jacks are unfortunately still flourishing, and even those special offers of Dutch-grown plants in the Sunday coloureds are seldom worth the so-called bargain price at which they are offered. The dealer referred to in the previous paragraph regularly used the letters F.R.H.S. after his name in his advertisement. This helped to delude the ignorant and the gullible for they imagined it added to his bona fides. All it indicated was that he had paid his, then, £2 annual subscription to the Royal Horticultural Society which supposedly elevated his position by being a Fellow of the Society as in F.R.C.S. for example.

Many who fell for his offers would imagine that to be a Fellow of the R.H.S. was as great a distinction as a Fellow of the Royal College of Surgeons.

This reminds me of the man I knew who bought a doctorate from an obscure American university. He used it to help sales of the many books published under his name, if not by his own efforts, on a wide variety of gardening subjects as well as to entice customers to buy plants he grew for sale, some of which he bought from me. On one occasion he drove up to where I was busily engaged with a visiting party and demanded to be served at once. 'Don't you know,' he said, 'I'm Doctor --------?' He was asked to go to the office where he should have gone in the first place and I learned afterwards that he had left without his request for plants being met, because he insisted on trade terms for what was in fact a small retail-sized order as previous ones had also been.

The Royal Horticultural Society is no longer a club for the elite in horticulture, as it was once reputed to be. Its ruling Council is now democratic and has a larger proportion of nurserymen members instead of mainly wealthy or influential amateurs and academics. Perhaps the period of transition had begun in 1931, in which year I was alloted a space of twelve feet by three feet on which to stage my first exhibit at the Chelsea Flower Show. But as a youngster I held in a certain awe the bowler-hatted bigwigs who, I was told, were Council members or holders of the Victoria Medal of Honour. This medal is the highest of the honours awarded by the Society and is restricted to 63 holders at any one time. They can legitimately add V.M.H. to their names. Some do, but some do not, and I am amongst the latter since being so honoured in 1971.

Now that my son Adrian, too, has been awarded the V.M.H. for his services to horticulture at the unusually early age of 45, he and I have the distinction of being the only father and son holders. He, in contrast to my first cap-in-hand request for space at Chelsea, plans exhibits there forty times the size to gain gold medals and praise for his artistry and the range and quality of his plants.

There was a time when to gain an R.H.S. award of merit for a new plant introduction came as a great fillip. But not any more. After about twenty or more such awards I came to believe that a good new plant would sell on its merits and that an award makes very little difference in the long run. Neither the system of judging after trial at the R.H.S. Wisley Garden in Surrey, nor the awards given spontaneously on the vote of the appropriate committee at the R.H.S. Hall or the Chelsea Flower Show are calculated to be fully indicative of the garden worthiness of a new plant.

I served on an R.H.S. committee for a few years but found that its twenty or so members were fully entitled to vote without regard to their familiarity with or knowledge of the type of plant being put up for award. This practice had such faults that I decided to resign, especially when one committee member made a certain overt request which niggled me. He had put up a number of plants for award, some of which had been overlooked although they were in cultivation. He made no bones about his objective. It was to beat the record of the greatest number of awards of merit gained by any proposer up to that time – as if this would be to his personal credit. No doubt he felt it would be, but the award is given, or should be, to the plant, not the proposer. Having some quite strong feelings on such a matter of principle, his request had to be ignored.

This experience tended to deter me from sending new or neglected garden-worthy plants for judging; but perhaps this is being unfair to plants which deserve to gain recognition. Perhaps also I am being somewhat eccentric in my attitude to plants generally. They are living subjects in their own right, part of nature's bounty. They will still be around when we mortals are no longer here, and I doubt if we have the right to consider them as our chattels or as inanimate objects, over which we have full rights of possession. Rather we should consider ourselves as their temporary custodians.

CHAPTER THIRTEEN

Then and Now

A man, according to the old adage, is as old as he feels. Those of us fortunate enough not to feel old, even if by our tally of years we are, have to make a series of mental adjustments. Reminders of age come from various sources, apart from such physical signs as tiring more quickly, being less nimble and the like. We tend to be reminded of age by the increasing number of our contemporaries who have passed on, and how aged those have become whom we have not seen for years, while the vast majority of the people we see are obviously younger than ourselves. It is the young who bring reminders that time must be nearly up for us, and that it is later than we care to think. Grandchildren fast becoming adults force us to draw conclusions.

The tendency of the old to look back with some affection on the past or to contrast it with the present may be harmless but the present is what really matters. For youth it is the future which counts for most. They see no merit in 'Lord teach us to number our days that we may apply our hearts unto wisdom.' This may be the belated prayer of the old, but it seldom appeals to the young who see only the benefits of progress stretching away into the seemingly limitless future.

Progress as we know it is largely in the field of technology, but a true assessment of progress must surely be whether or not it makes for better living. There is ample evidence, which we tend to ignore, that almost every advance has a debit as well as a credit side. The jet engine, nuclear power, computers and bulldozers can also be used to destroy, to limit freedom and employment and devastate vital forests. Small wonder then that some of us hark back to gentler, less thrusting times when people seemed to be more contented even if they lacked modern amenities and the money to spend on leisure enjoyment. It must be indicative of some malaise to reflect that now, when the vast majority never had it so good, the crime rate is many times greater than when times were lean.

Rural life has been affected most of all. Many villagers have foresaken the land, lured often by higher wages into the towns, but the influx of commuters and weekenders has made village populations soar. A labourer's cottage which could have been bought fifty years ago for two or three hundred pounds is likely to fetch twenty or thirty thousand now. Such crazy effects of inflation, to which we have to adapt in order to live, are probably with us for ever, as so-called progress races inexorably on, leaving some of us with a yearning for stability and some nostalgia for the best of times past.

But there, when the rising generation becomes old, they too will take much the same view as we do now. It has been going on for centuries, and we are not the first ones to hear those familiar laments, 'I don't know what things are coming to', and 'They wouldn't have got away with it in my young days'. But I can remember getting away with practices and escapades when young which would not be tolerated nowadays, such as saying I was twenty when I was eighteen in order to get a better paid and more responsible job. It causes me uneasy feelings when I reflect how brash, thrusting and opinionated I was at times. Even so, I worked on five different nurseries in less than five years and left each of my own accord. One head gardener at a stately home was friendly enough towards me to give me an early edition of William Robinson's *The English Flower Garden.* It was in two volumes, with every other page blank and on these I recorded not only my work as a propagator in a Tunbridge Wells nursery, but a few comments which were somewhat indiscreet. I still have these books, and, with more discretion since then, have never offered to let others borrow them.

Sixty years have passed since I last wrote in them, and memories come back of things I did not record. Of the greenhouse foreman, for example, who used to cajole other workers to relieve themselves into a bucket he kept for the purpose. His special pride was his begonias – the Lorraine and Petersen varieties for the Christmas trade, and he believed that matured human urine was the secret of his success. I hesitate to mention his name or that of a man I was told to help plant irises. He smoked a clay pipe and demonstrated how he made the fullest use of the black 'twist' tobacco he bought, then costing about eightpence an ounce. First he chewed it and then dried it before smoking. Having done so, he used the ash for snuff. At the same nursery, a lad of my own age virtually fell down on the job we shared twice a day, of taking off and replacing two hundred 6ft by 4ft pit lights. Back in the potting shed to recover, he was questioned by the foreman as to why he was so wan and weak and eventually revealed that his mother insisted on putting a spoonful of Glauber Salts in his tea every morning.

Memories reveal other scenes unlikely to recur. Of a boy having to do what was normally the work of a donkey. The donkey, kept in a paddock near a large private house, was used mainly in summer for pulling the lawn mower. It had specially made shoes of leather to avoid leaving hoof marks. But the donkey died and was buried, people said, outside the vinery greenhouse in keeping with the belief that such an additive for fertility was incomparable for fine grapes. So far as I know, the donkey was never replaced, but the boy who had to pull the heavy 36-inch mower instead was not to be envied, for it was a very large lawn, and he also had to hand weed all the gravel paths and the driveway to the front door.

Such helpers were essential in the old days. Percy Piper's father – also a Percy – began as a 'stick boy' at twelve years of age. The term came, no doubt, from his having to collect and break sticks for kindling at the big house or the vicarage. His wage was a shilling a week and he was at the beck and call of both the gardener and the cook-housekeeper, as the go-between for what the garden produced and what the household required. He had also to clean and polish the boots and shoes, and it paid to keep on the right side of the cook for the sake of titbits of food she could privily give him. In course of time he became a groom as well as under-gardener, and among the skills he acquired was vermin trapping and killing, mowing, hedge laying and pruning. He excelled as a vegetable grower. And he was still active at ninety years of age, although he retired from mole trapping for me at eighty-seven.

I do not believe that such as the Percy Pipers, father and son, have now become extinct. Herbert Smith, also mentioned, was another who 'kep a'doin'', and this zest for activity – seen also in Manny Shinwell, Mother Teresa and many, many more, springs from within the individual. It is what they feel they must do from inner compulsion, so far as their physical abilities allow. And they enjoy doing whatever they undertake. For them 'being' is 'doing'; a challenge, whether altruistic or otherwise, which has to be met regardless. Such people – as many of them women as men – will continue to emerge, and a large proportion, one can be fairly sure, will be devoted gardeners.

Times change and conditions of life are changing more swiftly than ever before. But basically human nature changes very slowly indeed. Adaption to changing circumstances of life and work does not amount to radical changes in our nature, as becomes apparent when people are under stress of various kinds. Generally speaking, though, attitudes to work are different to those of fifty years ago, when workers were less protected and cosseted than they are now. Fewer people, whatever their status, appear to have a high sense of responsibility and more do as little as possible for as much as they can get.

My memory goes back to the time when 'no work, no pay' was the accepted order between master and man. An employer could send his labourers away if they turned up for outdoor work on a wet morning, perhaps soaked already having walked a mile or two to work. Very few workers owned rain-proof coats and old corn sacks were often their only weather protection. After World War I there were old army greatcoats and boots for sale cheaply, but rubber 'wellies' did not come in until the mid-1920s. Until then it was hob-nail boots which cost half a week's pay or more. Working men usually bought new boots after harvest, and some old-timers had a crude method of ensuring a good fit for such stiff leathered footwear. A new pair would be soaked in water overnight and put on next morning to dry out by the end of the day, being thus encouraged to conform better to the wearer's foot shape.

If 'no work, no pay' was accepted, some agricultural or horticultural employers who found workers under-cover jobs in wet weather reaped some reward for such philanthropy. The cream of the workers would be theirs, and so the custom spread until it became more general practice except for piece workers. The latter were usually the hardest working of any landsmen. As a farmer before the advent of mechanical diggers and harvesters, I had many a session with men, and sometimes women, who were avid for piece work, be it ditch digging, singling, hoeing and harvesting sugar beet, as well as 'taking' the corn harvest. They were usually in gangs of four, one of them being the leader with whom I had to strike a bargain. They were skilled and honest in keeping to a bargain, which gave them at least twenty-five per cent more than they would have earned at day work rates.

In horticulture piece work was not so easy to arrange and never occurred in my own hardy plant nursery, though rose and tree nurserymen could practise it more readily. Now, the proliferation of mechanical devices has nearly eliminated it altogether, and this is one reason why so few farm labourers are employed. It is a chicken-egg syndrome. When living standards rose as a right along with higher wages, causing inflation, which, having begun, is self propagating and spiralling, so machines were invented to reduce labour costs. And now that farm and nursery workers are paid more than fifty times as much in wages as they received fifty years ago, farmers have had to dispense with manual labour almost entirely. Trade union officials have been declaring for years that workers are driven from the land because of low wages, while the employers argue with equal conviction that they have been forced to reduce staff by mechanising as statutory wages rose with inflation to an uneconomic degree.

Agricultural wages apply to horticulture also, but most nursery products are not adaptable to mechanisation. None the less, planting and potting machines had to come, and sprays against weeds are more commonly taking the place of hand hoeing and weeding.

In 1939 my Oakington nursery amounted to thirty-six acres of plants and there were thirty-six full-time staff, including two in the office. Now, at Bressingham there are about one hundred and fifty acres of plants and shrubs and well over two hundred staff. But for mechanical devices another fifty at least would be required for planting, potting and weed control. But on the five acres of nursery under my charge there are five full-time workers including myself, and one or two part timers. This is disproportionate to the ratio on the main nursery because we practise hand work almost entirely in producing mostly plants needing special care. As an old timer with an affection for the older methods – necessary in the circumstances – it is a joy for me to participate fully in this little nursery, with time to spare for the five acres of decorative garden, most of the maintenance of which falls to two devoted women helpers, Mary and Beryl. These cheerful, enthusiastic ladies, with families who have grown up, have been with me for about ten years. They put in twenty-four hours a week from February to December, and prefer to take an exclusive and prideful attitude to the garden. Since Percy Piper retired in 1983, Peter Sare has taken over seed raising and sowing as well as responsibility for what is grown in rows, some garden re-grouping and the trials of hostas and other subjects. He came straight from school in 1964 and has never worked on the main nursery. Under him come two younger men, Derrick and David, as does Sid – a retired road-roller driver who digs, plants or hoes three days a week. Stella, also full time, is concerned with indoor plants, plant centre orders and sales, and stock records. She came back after a twelve-year absence.

These are the people who help me to run the garden and the little nursery, and while there is full liaison between us and the main nursery, there is virtually no interchange of staff. The enclave runs as smoothly as can be with only frost and snow holding up the routine of seasonal work outdoors. It is my job to scheme ways and means of keeping abreast and I try to keep the others in the picture so that they know what to expect. There is never a period when plants are not being handled, although I am the only one at work during the long break at Christmas and New Year. As on the main nursery, large quantities of dormant plants are lifted in December so as to have them on hand to divide or propagate should severe weather come. Hostas, astilbes, rodgersias, hemerocallis and others can be stored for weeks for winter division, whilst phlox, papavers and so on can be propagated from root cuttings from December to March.

By March, orders are taking priority. Three hundred retail orders daily are despatched in the main packing shed and since we grow about four hundred kinds for the nursery, my four full-time helpers have to go round the beds lifting by the labels Peter sorts over according to location. A 'round' takes on average two hours and two rounds per day are often required. This is not my job, for I am busy dividing or otherwise propagating or planting in the garden. My main job is to keep the seasonal routine going with trays full of stock for next year's requirements. Some kinds require a two-year programme. Plants such as adonis, *Liriope muscari,* kniphofias and several more need to be two years old to make good dividable plants, and this means having two batches of each kind. In the case of trilliums it takes even longer and the queen of them all, the double white trillium takes five or six years to produce a saleable plant, while single-flowered species take almost as long from seed. In a general way, spring flowering plants (beginning with adonis, trilliums and others), are the first to be lifted, propagated and replanted in early autumn, laying in those required for orders separately. So the season really begins in August, with *Adonis amurensis*, which flowers before winter ends.

The autumn lifting season for orders extends over a ten-week period and planting has to fit in with maybe up to one hundred and fifty 'rounds' for the packing shed in trailers behind a mini-tractor. The planting method is that of digging to a row-line, with a spade cut against it, and when plants have been set with their roots well down, digging covers them until enough room has been made for the next row. It is the slow way, but it is still the surest, and when required farmyard manure is dug in, as well as sand to improve the soil's texture. To plant three or four acres in this way is a costly job, but most of the plants are worth it. The machine planting of some has been tried and heavy losses have been the result.

It falls on me to decide on what to plant, when and how and where, as well as to prepare most of the material for the planters. Another dimension has recently been added to our commitments. The new retail plant centre needs to be supplied with potted stock drawn from our little department because this is where many unusual kinds are grown. So now, to some extent in my retirement, I have gone back to much the same kind of work that I was doing over fifty years ago. A new 15ft by 15ft potting shed has been built for us, and several thousands of plants in wide variety are lifted and potted to augment those grown on the main nursery. I enjoy making up the potting compost by hand as well as the potting, especially when it's wet or windy outside.

Sometimes I wonder if I have become a workaholic. The compulsion I feel to work long hours, while I have the energy to do so, is not a vital necessity in order to make a living. The choice is entirely mine so to do.

It is just my way of life and I would find the onset of some physical disability which forced inactivity upon me very hard to cope with. But the inevitable is inescapable and this encourages me to live each day as it comes and make the most of it thankfully and joyfully, but for a few niggling worries – about inclement weather, inexplicable plant losses, insidious weeds and oddly, perhaps, a few incongruous noises.

Fifty years ago one heard more noises from cattle and – at Oakington – steam trains. The bells from the nearby Bressingham church used to annoy me, but now they seldom ring except for the chiming clock which keeps remarkably good time. What angers me is the hellish roar of fighter planes, but the noise of the big lorries on the main road is much less disturbing and menacing. The mower's whine for several hours a week in summer tends to impinge and my grandson Jason is learning to play the electric guitar. His parents naturally insist on him practising in the open-doored garage – close enough for me at work to hear every note. And though a learner, he would probably top any competition for the weirdest noises which this instrument is capable of making.

But one learns, with age, to be more tolerant, to live and let live. Peace of mind is the prime need, for with that the zest for life can still flourish. Those of us with an abiding love for plants and gardening are scarcely conscious of any loss of zest. It takes on a somewhat different shape if our early life was concerned largely with an ambition to succeed professionally, but with age, the stimulus plants provide, and the constant challenge their cultivation gives, is enough to keep this zest alive.

CHAPTER FOURTEEN

Gardeners and Gardening

It is said that Adam was the first gardener. This is rather questionable. It is more likely that he was assumed to be the first, his habitat being the Garden of Eden. If, having disobeyed the Lord God, he became a gardener in order to live – 'By the sweat of thy brow shalt thou eat bread' – so he gardened under duress. So do some of his descendants today. In some circumstances such gardening can be interesting and satisfying. It is possible for those on the poverty line to grow food crops out of necessity, if they have a plot to cultivate and find the effort worth while. Satisfaction comes in such cases as a reward for labour, using skill and muscle to make the soil yield some of the necessities of life they might not otherwise be able to afford. To reap full reward, however, their need is to tackle each job with some enthusiasm, working with nature and with some thankfulness for small mercies. Such people are also endowed with a certain pride, for to give up or slack off would be letting themselves down as well as their plot.

I am old enough to remember when such gardeners were not uncommon. During and between the wars, low wages or food shortages may have acted as a spur, but once the challenge of the cottage home plot or allotment was accepted, the work done and the produce grown was evidence enough of satisfaction and success. There were two outstanding examples I can give from more recent years. Herbert Smith had worked for me at Oakington, retiring only when he reckoned his own cottage garden was enough to keep him busy. He grew flowers, fruit and vegetables despite heavy soil to as near perfection as possible and remained active until he was well past ninety. When I asked what was his secret, he replied, 'Keep a'doin' –

just keep a'doin'.' Percy Piper senior also worked for me and kept a quite large garden going, as well as mole trapping at well past eighty. What surpluses he had he sold or gave away. Waste of space was for him a sin and he became artful by the time he too was ninety, in avoiding waste of effort. He was a schemer as well as a doer in his gardening, in order to make the most of his plot, and that of his decrepit neighbour, with the least effort and to the greatest effect.

The spirit motivating such gardeners is really little different from that of those who are well off and need only garden for beauty's sake. Enthusiasm, supported by skill and determination, are the essentials to become a true gardener. Knowledge can be acquired – and surely will accumulate with practice. The surest way of learning is often the hard way, and knowledge thus acquired is unlikely to be forgotten, which is more than could be said for book learning and the advice given by others, however expert they presume to be. And, as Charles Kingsley wrote, one needs only to be enthusiastic about something to avoid being bored. A true gardener is certainly never bored because a garden can provide all the interest one needs, if it is large enough to hold a constant challenge to strive for perfection. Even a quite small plot can be a challenge in striving for the maximum display or variety possible within its confines.

It has been my privilege to have many true gardeners as friends for life. Herbert Smith and Percy Piper (father to Percy the 'fiddling' hybridiser mentioned in Chapter Thirteen) were quite lowly in the accepted social scale. At the high end the late Sir David Scott stands out as a true gardener. He died in 1986 at ninety-nine years of age. His gardening days came to an end only shortly before his death, but even when his body had to give in to infirmity his mind was as alert as ever. He made a shrub garden on his allotted share of the family estate at Boughton near Kettering a very long time ago. Not for him the aristocratic pride of ordering others to do the heavy, menial tasks. He enjoyed doing them himself, as well as the planting, pruning and even the weeding. I came to know, to respect and to enjoy his company after he married another indefatigable, dedicated gardener, Valerie Finnis. To stay overnight with them, as I did on several occasions, was a delight. Both were specialists, yet were able to merge their respective interests. Sometimes their individualism sparkled with the kind of banter that was a delight to hear. They mostly worked separately, Valerie on her immense range of alpines and Sir David on his shrubs, and both had boundless enthusiasm.

On one occasion I walked up the steps to their gardens to find David on his knees hand-weeding the gravel path that led from Valerie's garden to his own. At over ninety he had to be careful of his game hip and this was a job that did him no harm, he explained, especially as he had an aversion to weed-killers. When his disability worsened to make those steps more difficult to mount, he had materials brought into the back premises of the Dower House in which they lived, so that he could deal with cuttings or seedlings of Valerie's alpines, just for love and with the same 'Keep a'doin'' spirit expounded by Herbert Smith to me. For me, such men have been and are an inspiration.

Nor must I omit to mention my own father whose love of gardening kept him busy. Latterly he worked to restore the neglected Rectory garden where he lived to be close to my sister. That garden he took up as a challenge at the age of eighty-three and he enjoyed it until he overtaxed his strength at the age of eighty-six cutting back an overgrown hedge. This put an end to his lifelong dedication to gardening for love and beauty. He was meticulous in being a tidy gardener. He liked orderliness, never begrudging the extra time and effort it took. And although he was one of the hardest workers I ever knew, now and then he would pause to stand and stare at the beauty of a scene or to admire a single flower. And he would spend wet days and dark evenings painting flowers just for love as if to keep in touch.

It may be purely incidental, but several of the true gardeners I know, or have known, themselves live quite frugally. David and Valerie were in the habit of taking a few sandwiches or bread and cheese into a hut in the shrub garden to save time and trouble over lunch. The slope and steps down to their house was some deterrent, no doubt, but there was more to it than that. They had very little paid help and both preferred to do without it whenever possible. It was thus also with my father. I never knew him to shirk a task, however hard or tedious it was, and I have sometimes taken my cue from him in working alongside paid helpers inclined to take it easy in order to set the pace. And it has also come back in a roundabout way that some helpers much preferred not to work alongside me for this same reason.

This is by the way, for it comes to mind that my sister Kay is a fair example of another type of true gardener. Her plot is decidedly in keeping with what has become known as the cottage garden. As a freelance portrait painter and water colour artist, she lives frugally out of necessity, having never married. At eight-three years of age she is as active as ever and I believe still rides her moped when needing to go shopping. Her garden surrounds her little house and she tends it lovingly, higgledy-piggledy though it is by some standards. The soil is dry and chalky, but things grow for her. Not that she craves for choice kinds, but rather to mass flowers which appeal most to her with no spaces wasted. She likes scented flowers and has lots of pinks and polyanthus, interspersed if need be with annuals. And she also grows her own salad crops, but flowers come first.

What is it, I often wonder, that inspires some people to become devoted gardeners while others garden only when they have to and a few totally abhor gardening and refuse even to do a stroke. Not long since I walked the length of a street in Norwich where continuous rows of Victorian houses on both sides had little fenced in plots behind railing-topped walls, with wicker gates through which to reach the front door. The only uniformity of these plots – about six feet by twelve feet – was their size. Their contents were anything but uniform. Some were cared for with a rose or two, edging plants or bedding plants. Some sported a miniature lawn, others an ornament including a gnome cemented down to deter theft. Sea shells and curiously shaped flints were also seen as ornamental edging. In some, perennial plants were flowering in orderly, cared for array, but in others plants had wildly taken over, or the whole plot apart from the path was given over to some ground-covering subject. But for every cared-for garden there must have been at least one that was totally neglected, with rank weeds – thistles, ragwort or docks, and rosebay a menace for the seeds they distributed around. Here was a cross-section of what gardening meant to the occupiers. A quarter of the plots perhaps were cared for, their owners making the best of a tiny plot. Another quarter were, it would seem, undedicated, doing what they had to but no more; while the remainder were either not interested or totally against any attempt to interfere with nature, and oblivious of the weeds' nuisance to others.

Such examples of widely differing attitudes to gardening can be seen wherever one looks for them – they occur in every grade of the social order and do not appear to be linked in any way to wealth or poverty. There must, however, be people who, if they had the means, would enjoy some form of gardening – and might do so even if restricted to a few house plants. I once read of a lady who, as a substitute for curtains at a window, grew a collection of epiphyte orchids in great variety hanging down from above. And, at the opposite end of the scale, there are owners of plenty of garden space who make no attempt to beautify it. The answer to the question of why people are so different in their attitude to gardening must lie in the labyrinthine realms of human psychology. Those who are devoid of any interest can scarcely be accused of not possessing some need to care and nurture or to come closer to nature, because there are other pursuits by which such urges can be fostered.

There is no point in trying to analyse the differences in people's approach to gardening, much less to be critical of those who find some other means of recreation and self expression, or to express what creativeness they possess. It is more relevant to speculate on what inspires those to whom gardening is an important if not a vital need, and what it means to different people. It cannot be said to be an attribute of a certain type of person, rather that it provides an outlet to part of a many-sided nature. It crops up in tycoons and politicians, priests and criminals, and I am quite certain that, for some people, it comes as a means of sublimation – an outlet for self expression otherwise choked or suppressed. Not everyone is aware of any creativeness latent within themselves, nor if they have that kind of spark do they feel compelled to foster it. Nevertheless, I believe most people are born with such a propensity even if only a few are encouraged or allowed to develop it.

Even if no more than half the population of Britain has any interest in gardening, it stands far and away above any other means or method of recreation which allows individual creativeness to emerge. What makes it even more valuable and distinctive is that both sexes can indulge on the basis of equality. It might be said that gardening comes more naturally to women than to men, but one can only guess that women gardeners are in the majority. What is even more likely is that in remotest times women were the first to cultivate the soil, while men

did the hunting and fighting. And even today there are far more
women land workers than men in some countries, though this may not
be from choice. Keeping to Britain – high ranking as it is among
countries where gardening for love is practised – there's little difference
between men and women when it comes to gardening fame, at least
since emancipation got under way.

A belief that continues to gain strength to my way of thinking is that
the appeal of gardening to both men and women has links with the
androgyny in human nature. It allows the caring and nurturing
feminine element in the male to find expression, though this comes
more naturally, of course, to women. It comes also as an outlet to the
creativeness latent in both sexes in widely varying measure, but all in all
gardening is a means of striking some kind of balance between the
masculine and feminine elements present in both sexes from birth,
although restrictions and conditionings during childhood may warp or
hinder its natural development. A man is more likely than a woman to
be expansive in his gardening, to make features and introduce trees and
shrubs where space permits. He may also care for tiny plants or go in
for exotics, but the woman is more likely to be green fingered, to rear
plants lovingly and to look upon them somewhat as her children. I
would guess that gardening folk generally show a higher ratio of
'wholeness' and fulfilment in the art of living than any other section of
the community. These generalisations cannot be very wide of the truth.
Maybe I am out of my depth in such theorising, but it is a facet of a
phenomenon which some thought has evoked, and until or unless
someone better qualified than I comes up with a more rational
explanation I much prefer to stick to what I believe is true.

The type of gardener for whom I have least respect is the one who
makes no personal effort other than to pay the bills and wages. So-
called landscape gardeners, or garden architects, thrive on people who
have the means but not the will or incentive to plan or to do a hand's
turn themselves. There are, of course, those who feel incompetent to
plan and construct and plant, but are willing enough to maintain a
garden and may even make good gardeners as they work and learn. At
the other end of the scale there are those who are bone lazy when it
comes to manual work, but some of these probably use up their
energies in sports and games. It is those, whether wage or salary

earners, in business or even unemployed, for whom manual work is anathema, who find life becomes empty and sterile as their physical capabilities decline or become atrophied. Such a waste of positive living is, alas, endemic since it has always been a feature of any organised society.

Human body movement is activated they say by the brain, which in turn is prompted by the mind – the self or will. So many people nowadays have to earn a living by using their brains and fingers rather than their body muscles. When they feel the need to do so they go in for other means of exercise from games to jogging, and apart from having to do some walking, they hold back unused much of their potential physical energy. For most of us both body and brain are underused and undervalued so far as potential is concerned. This is not the healthiest way to live and now we see leisure referred to as an industry – which strikes me as being rather a contradiction in terms. But we have freedom of choice or nearly so, and it is this freedom, the ability to decide how we use our brains and bodies, which stamps our superiority over the rest of the animal kingdom, which lacks individual self consciousness. What other animals do with their bodies is motivated by instinct or compulsion (witness domestic animals) but because we have choice and are able to make decisions, it comes as both a privilege and a responsibility to make good use of our special human attributes.

This applies, surely, in the way we use our free time, having the choice of doing nothing – and being merely entertained is seldom a worthy pastime – or using our brains to activate our bodies usefully, and then, having done a reasonable stint, to relax in one way or another. Some regularity in using our free time is an advantage, but the greatest purpose of all lies in accomplishment. And the finest recreational means of using brain and body in order to live a wholesome life is by working with what nature has provided – the soil and the infinite variety it will produce if we play our part. No matter whether it is producing food or creating beauty and providing mental refreshment and interest, there is no better way to use our free time. Our minds expand, our brains keep alert and our bodies keep in trim if we use them sensibly and purposefully in keeping with our physical abilities. No pundit seems able to prove irrefutably that life has a purpose, divine or otherwise; but we can be sure that to live fully, to use our respective gifts and abilities both physical and mental, is the right way and most likely to bring its own reward in this life. The Parable of the Talents told by Jesus speaks volumes to us if we chose to heed.

To cap the above unsolicited and maybe unwelcome lapse into moralising, I still maintain that there is no recreational pursuit to compare with gardening for keeping one's mind and body in tune with one another and with nature. The manual work involved uses all the muscles – not all the time perhaps, because seasonal tasks call on different muscle usage. Digging comes during the autumn and winter when most energy is required to promote bodily warmth, while summer hoeing and weeding are just right in keeping us supple. Wheeling a barrow as well as sowing and planting is no more likely than any other exercise to cause backache, and one is just as likely to slip a spinal disc by the mildest of exertions as by heaving out a tree stump. But apart from being good exercise for the body, gardening exercises the brain as well. Almost every task is better accomplished by using one's head as well. There is the hopeful anticipation of a job well done which requires thought and there is a need for a watchful eye for pests and diseases appearing. Even straightforward digging and hoeing calls for skill, and skill can only come from thoughtful practice.

The one regular task which calls for the minimum of thought and considerable effort, if manually performed, is mowing the lawn. It is also the outstanding example of a task meriting the use of a machine for its easement. Apart from acquiring a little tractor rather than a barrow for a large garden, I would say that any machine other than a lawn mower and possibly a hedge clipper is a bad investment. Mechanical diggers and cultivators are of worse than dubious value. If perennial weeds are in their path, the rotary-bladed machine will propagate rather than destroy – especially couch grass. If the soil is wet or heavy they will churn it up messily, and where it is light leave the top few inches too fine and often uneven. And they will tend to make a hard pan form at the point of deepest penetration. It is true that they will scurry over and kill off a bare strip where annual weeds are young and menacing, but that is about the limit of their usefulness in my experience from first using one in 1934. It is very rarely that I borrow one from the main nursery nowadays for use on my own little adjoining nursery where hand-work is the general rule for both planting and hoeing. I have also used the plough type and those that scuffle with rigid tines, but only the latter has occasionally done a useful job.

My conviction that manual work is best is not based solely on the benefit it brings to those who are not reluctant to use their brains and muscles, but that the latter will give far better results than a mechanical device. Most of them are smelly and noisy anyway, emitting fumes to pollute the air breathed in by the operator. It should be mentioned that the noisiest, if not the smelliest, machine sometimes used in my gardening domain is a chain saw. I have to admit that I am willing to put up with its faults because it is so effective compared with a crosscut saw which took two men an hour to fell a tree which a chain saw could do in five or ten minutes. All the same, I use a bow saw quite often for trimming and heavy pruning beyond the capacity of pruning tools. There was a time when I delighted in using an axe, but now it comes in only for severing tree roots, thus making it permanently blunt.

Of all the manual tasks the one I like least and am apt to neglect is staking or otherwise supporting perennials which cannot be relied upon to stand up unaided. The stage of growth at which this is best done calls not only for vigilance but prompt action if need be. Neglect in acting at the right time can make the job take much longer and may be ineffective if strong winds and rain come just as growth is beginning to become top heavy. The time to give supports is, of course, when it is still sturdy and upright – and this is likely to be well in advance of flowering time, especially with such weak-stemmed subjects as delphiniums. As a chore the necessary sticks or whatever have to be prepared well in advance so you can tackle the job without first having to find or trim them. There are wire supports available which can be used year after year, but to rely upon sticks which are not to hand when required in May is likely to delay the job until it is too late.

It was this dislike of staking which set me off to find a less troublesome means of growing perennials to better advantage, and to my wholehearted preference for island beds. No other means of display had ever occurred to me than that of the conventional one-sided herbaceous border until one year I omitted to put in supports until it was too late to remedy the damage an early June gale caused. This, and the fact that perennials in which I specialised were losing out in favour of less labour-intensive plants, aided by several gardening scribes, became an urgent challenge. Both mine and other borders I had seen emphasised groups for massed display. To achieve it, the plants were crammed in to the exclusion of light and air, for which every plant competed. The result was weakened stem growth and excessive height as plants became drawn up. The backing fence also reduced light and air and encouraged growth to lean away from it, and this, in turn, made the taller kinds at the rear overhang the shorter ones at the front. Apart from all this, close planting designed to give masses of colour with a minimum of bare soil showing in between made access for weeding and staking very difficult.

These factors soon became seen as faults inherent in borders, a trend begun, it was said, by William Robinson of Gravetye in Victoria's time, as a break from bedding. It became a popular form of gardening for almost a century, but during most of that period labour was cheap and plentiful. In front of my house was a large lawn and here was the obvious place to try out ways and means of allowing plants to grow more as nature intended – in island beds, a term I thought up as I had not seen these beds employed elsewhere. It was simply a matter of carving out from the sward shapes to fit in with the informal environment of a shelter belt and trees, to be viewed as a whole from the house. In a general way groups of tall plants were located in the centre parts of each bed, and heights were then graded down towards the perimeter, where subjects of only a few inches in height formed edging groups. And, if individual plants within a group were spaced to give a massed display, ample space was left around, between it and adjoining groups. The whole idea was to allow plenty of light and free circulation of air, with colours blending and forms interspersed.

It worked. The first season was decidedly encouraging but the second, when the plants reached maturity, was convincing. An added bonus came not only from easier access, but less than ten per cent of them needed support because growth was shorter and sturdier, and because one had all round vision of the bed's contents – from wherever one stood. Although I have been credited as the inventor of island beds, I would make no such claim. Someone, somewhere, sometime must have surely used perennials in beds with all round access. But perhaps they did not trouble to proclaim their advantages in a way that others might follow, for nowadays the media – and especially television – are able to feature fresh approaches to gardening. For me, it was vital that I should become a propagandist because I produced hardy plants for a living, though at that time, the 1950s and early 1960s, my business was strictly wholesale only. Hardy plants were also my love and there could be no question of switching over to shrubs and ground coverers in order to produce and sell what was in greatest demand to profit thereby.

CHAPTER FIFTEEN

Towards Harmony

Peace, so Litvinov declared before the cold war began, is indivisible. So too must harmony be in a more intimate sense, and harmony, or lack of it, shows up in gardens as well as in human relations. In a garden, however, harmony has two aspects. They are quite different and seldom easy to reconcile when seeking to form an overall view. One aim is to create a garden which is in harmony with its surroundings, and this is the more difficult because such surroundings might be outside one's property and therefore one's control. If they are, then if harmony is an objective it has to be on a smaller scale to ensure that no part of what is under one's control is out of keeping with the rest.

The vast majority of gardens comes within this latter category, because of boundary restrictions, which in some cases might be veritable eyesores such as ugly buildings, or even a wall or fence. The most usual garden plot is a rectangle at the rear of the house, and the narrower it is the more restricted are the possibilities of achieving harmony with its surroundings. Yet it is possible to make such a garden a kind of oasis in which harmony reigns by careful design and planning, and by selecting plants which will fill it with beauty. Some screening subjects around the perimeter enable the owner to concentrate on achieving harmony within.

Those condemned to confine their gardening to an oblong strip like those of their neighbours on either side, usually seek privacy. The tendency then is to plant a hedge or something to break the view of a fence or wall, and to front it with borders so as to leave space for a lawn between. A patio or rose bed might appeal, close to the house, and space may be left at the far end in which to grow fruit or vegetables. All very practical, no doubt, but harmony plays little or no part in such a layout, especially if a garden shed, bean poles or raspberry canes come into the picture when viewed from the house.

Harmony, however, like beauty, is in the eye of the beholder. Some people, indeed many people, would not find such a view out of harmony or in any way offensive, especially if they have put lots of colourful plants in the borders. Their eyes would be drawn to where the colour is and a deck chair on the patio or lawn might induce all the harmony and contentment they feel they need. Nor should they be criticised, if their aesthetic sensibilities do not stir them to greater efforts to achieve such an objective. A garden should be a place in which to allow the mind to relax from cares and stresses. But there are some who, with a genuine love for plants and a more acute sense of harmony would be discontented, with a longing to make a typical garden plot more interesting, more satisfying than its limitations would appear to allow. And it might not be at all easy to break with convention, especially if husband or wife (or vice versa) discourages radical change in the layout, one being a keen gardener but not the other, as is often the case.

While a break with the conventional layout is probably necessary, it does not mean that one has to scrap what is already there and begin again from scratch. Nor does it mean that the aim should be to go in for beds with lots of curves, or to try to defeat the straight lines within which the plot is constrained. This cannot be done and would defeat any attempt at harmony for if such straight-line boundaries prevail, then no amount of informality of design within them will achieve such a purpose. The aim should be to concentrate on achieving harmony in the space between these boundaries with beds or borders containing plants which are in harmony with each other. Such an aim is unlikely to be achieved in one season but is much more likely to be successful if accomplished bit by bit, as skill and imagination go along with knowledge. It might well prove in these circumstances to be of absorbing interest and could be good fun at no great cost. Such interest can be infectious.

Here are a few suggestions on how to get away from convention. Assuming the garden strip is fairly level and that it is at the rear of the house, stand and stare at the view. The compass direction is of some importance at this stage because, if facing north, account must be taken of the house shadow and where to locate a sunny spot for sitting out. If other than between north-east and north-west, the focus point should settle for a position about half way to the far end. That is where the main area for a collection of plants or dwarf shrubs should be. Beyond it would be the place for taller shrubs – some evergreens, including conifers, and a flowering tree or two such as cherries, always with the tallest at the rear and well spaced to allow for growth. In between can be grown perennials which can tolerate some shade.

The main bed should come next, taking up the whole width of the plot except for screening subjects against the boundary, with a path, preferably paved, on three sides. The remaining side nearest the house needs no path because here is the lawn, making the main bed an island. Its size would be a matter of choice, but should not be skimpy because it is designed to become the focal point, the bed which holds maximum appeal, not only for its position (just beyond the middle distance), but because of what it contains – a collection of perennials in the widest possible variety. If space allows, have three each of slow-growing plants and the dwarfest to group round the edges, but only one clump each of such kinds as kniphofia, which become large. The grading of expected heights should allow for the tallest to be beyond the half-way mark, coming down steeply behind. And between them and the rear path should be dwarfish, early-flowering kinds to be seen before the taller ones attain much height to obscure the view.

The bed would be best as a rectangle – perhaps with rounded corners on the lawn side to make grass mowing easier. Straight lines do not harmonise with informal curves. If a design on these lines reduces lawn space too much, it can be widened to come almost up to the screening hedge or whatever is in front of the boundary. There may be existing conventional borders on either side of the lawn next to the boundary and more than likely they are unsatisfactory. So often plants which are over-tall in relation to the width of the borders create an unpleasing effect, and it would be far better to use these narrow strips for shrubs which would form a screen, though not so dense as to prevent neighbours from peering through to admire the harmonious transformation one has achieved.

A north-facing plot could include a bed shaded by the house. There could also be a bed for shade-loving plants on the north side of the taller shrubs and trees at the far end of a south-facing garden. This is to say that the shade factor lends itself to the use of a different range of plants, including some of great charm. But near a south-facing rear of a house there are roses and irises, as well as a low, raised bed for alpine plants to consider, if space allows, all giving scope for variety.

There is a tendency for modern houses nowadays to follow the American pattern of having more garden in front of the house than at the back. With these a greater compromise is necesssary to achieve harmony. The view has to be considered in reverse, as seen from the road, because the road itself has no place in a harmonious background view seen from the house. Nor can privacy be achieved at all easily. If privacy is obtainable only behind the house, where there is too little garden space to accommodate a collection of interesting plants, then a collection has to be placed between house and road with, perhaps, the risk of pilfering. One's sensitivity in regard to harmony has to be concentrated even more on what can be achieved in a confined space, taking as much account of the surroundings as possible. Avenue or other trees, as well as the house, may cast shadows which could enable a good collection of suitably adaptable plants to be grown, including hostas, astilbes, hemerocallis and lots of dwarf subjects, which would do well in semi-shade given good soil and watering facilities in periods of dryness. One must, however, be aware that some trees have far-reaching roots which would be a menace, and two of the most popular, birch and beech, are in this category. Fortunate indeed are those with gardens having already a pleasing background of trees, these far enough away to induce no worries about their root spread.

But first some advice to those with a small formal garden plot on a slope. In the case of a rear garden with an upward slope, it is easier to plan on the lines suggested for a level plot, with perhaps less necessity for screening. But almost any slope lends itself to a terrace at some point or other, and, if built correctly with suitable materials, will have the effect of adding to the space for plants, or be ornamental in itself with no loss of harmony. But terracing would be quite expensive unless one is prepared to tackle its construction alone. Bricks or stone of a soft shade, and preferably old, can be effective, and planting holes could be left between them. Wall plants and climbers can be of assistance. The shade factor is important, and a north-facing wall looks well with shade-loving plants in a bed at its foot. A terrace wall retaining a slope should itself slope a little against the earth behind to give it stability.

My own garden has slopes here and there, mainly resulting from ancient clay digging for brick making, and has many walls. These walls total some three hundred yards in length and from one foot to four feet in height. I built them all over several years with Norfolk flints, having had no previous building experience. Having developed a knack of fitting such irregular stones together so that the best face of each faces the front with a minimum of cement showing, I found it a fascinating pastime. This type of wall building is not so good for leaving crevices in which plants can grow, and the different shapes and shades of colour of the stones are pleasing enough not to hide with climbers or tall plants. It was slow work, for not only does one have to find stones to fit, but also it is necessary to let the cement of the last-laid course dry out before placing another course on top. Also one has to make both the front and top-facing surfaces reasonably smooth. It became work I enjoyed so much that I looked around to find a place where another wall could be built to enhance the garden.

As a site in which harmony could reign, our park-like meadow was close to being ideal, but for the absence of a little stream or a natural pool or pond. But I cannot boast that what I contrived achieved all the harmony which could or should have been attained. Each island bed was sited with harmony in mind, to fit in with the mature trees and with the slopes. Each new bed, over a period of five years, was first marked out with sticks. Then I would walk all round at a distance to imagine the area filled with flowering and foliage plants, and how it would fit in with the rest in terms of background and proximity. Almost invariably I would go back and vary the position of the sticks and then repeat the performance until satisfied, before chopping up the turf and digging the bed. Later I saw the need for a shelter from showers, rather than a summerhouse, but it took me months before deciding just where to place it. In building it of flints, round and thatched, it followed no traditional design, but the final effect was not unpleasing, at least for me.

Apart from a shelter belt of oaks, elms and hollies on the north side of the garden, which, though straight, had outgrown formality, all the rest lent itself I believed to informality of design. Nothing was put on paper, for it was much better to develop it as a garden by careful on-site study. Someone once paid me the dubious compliment of asking if I had employed a garden architect to lay it out. But if I have no formal qualifications in that direction, no visitor has seen fit to criticise (to my face at any rate) what I have done. I am, however, self critical in that I am never satisfied with it. By this I mean not so much the layout as the placing of its contents. Several conifers have already been taken out when they became too large. They looked well for a few years, some with alpines between, but they gradually became more and more out of place. As does a fir, *Abies grandis*, still flourishing except for losing little branches when severe gales come. The fact is that I planted it as a specimen in an over-exposed position in 1961. Then it was four feet high, but now it is fifty or more feet tall and stands out like a monstrosity, increasingly offensive to the eye, taking up space and giving unwanted shade. It will have to come out when I can no longer tolerate it, but I dread the gap it will leave and have a fear of regret in missing its prominence.

Focal points in a large garden are of value, but should not be over done anywhere. They serve to draw the eye towards the spot where most interest lies and away from any external disharmony. In making my garden I sheered away from contriving an overall view, with focal points here and there, in favour of vistas. Three of these came about naturally for there were three entrances to the main part of the garden, but a fourth came as a surprise to visitors when the low-lying 'Dell' came into view from above.

Had I been confined to a smaller area – or had more time to devote to it – I would have been able to study harmony in closer detail, by means of plant association in a given space. As it was, the numerous and quite large island beds had to serve their main purpose of accommodating a wide collection of plants. More often than not where harmony was achieved it was more a matter of chance than design. True, I was careful to avoid clashes of colour and other errors, because I knew in advance the essentials of colour, height, spread and flowering time, even if only approximately. Nevertheless, errors were made and notes taken led to switchings at the next planting season. Only in a few instances was a deliberate effort made to plant a few kinds in association, with harmony between them fully in mind. And for all the extra joy it gives to appreciate plant combinations of grace and beauty, I have tended to rely on harmony being best served on a large scale, mainly because there has been too little time to practise it in closer detail.

It has to be said that no radical change from conventional modes, nor beginning from scratch on a clear site, is likely to achieve perfect harmony in one, or even two, seasons. It can scarcely be other than an expanding exercise, except where the plot is so small that only a few special favourites can be grown. But it is in deciding to begin in a comparatively small way, that the first results of making, and placing, a limited selection of plants will be rewarding enough to expand outwards from an initial project, until the birth of an idea becomes a fully matured reality. Even if it takes a few years to achieve all this, each year will add to the reward. This is all very well, some may say, but how does one begin selecting and placing plants in harmonious association?

To some, harmony is achieved by associating plants with different habits or type of growth against a background which enhances the view of the whole. For example, a shapely hosta with good foliage – green, glaucous-blue or variegated, may be surrounded by dwarfer flowering plants in which colours blend or contrast effectively. The choice would depend somewhat on soil and situation, and whether moist or shady, dry or sunny. If the latter, then a specimen or two of kniphofia, hemercallis, heuchera, phygelius and so on would best be interspersed with dianthus, gentian, campanula or achillea. Larger sunny beds provide scope to widen the variety of plants in the collection, but always imposing limits on expected heights in relation to the area involved. Tall perennials should be avoided unless there the bed has ample depth and width, then placing the tallest plants in the centre part of an island bed or at the rear of a one-sided border.

Another interpretation of a sense of harmony is to choose only those subjects which have both good foliage and spikey or sprayed flowers – where flowering is secondary to foliage effect and shapeliness. It might be preferred to restrict a bed or border to say favourite colour – blues and whites, blues and pinks, reds and yellows, and so on, or go in solely for grey- and silver-foliaged plants. The permutations are many. If no fixed ideas occur, then there is the opportunity to experiment in the knowledge that, by this means, preferences and an increasing appreciation of harmony will emerge. Mistakes and changes of mind can easily be remedied and give rise to knowledge and experience. A developing sense of harmony can also be achieved by studying plants and plant associations to be seen in the many gardens open to the public. Such study will also reveal how infinite is the variety of plants in existence, most of which are available from specialist nurseries.

Being dedicated to perennials, including alpines, shrubs have for me been very much a secondary interest. In recent years I have made no attempt to widen my knowledge of them, having become increasingly aware of how much I still have to learn about my own speciality. I am not, therefore, in a position to offer advice to those who wish to achieve greater harmony with the shrubby subjects they grow or may wish to grow. Adrian has given much thought to and has experimented much in this area, and especially to their use in association with conifers and heathers. I must admit that, at the intermediate stage of a few years from planting, they can be very effective together. Problems do arise, however, when heathers become straggly and conifers too large. Heathers are not adaptable to all kinds of soil and would have to be restricted in a general way to non-chalky soils. But other dwarf shrubs could take their place to complement conifers, just as the latter could give way in some measure to other shrubs or dwarf trees where space is restricted.

As a subject, harmony in the garden is capable of filling a complete book, but my sketchy notes may be of some help. It is so much a matter of carrying out one's individual notions of what constitutes a harmonious association in keeping, as far as possible, with the prevailing surroundings. Where this cannot be achieved because they offer no scope for inclusion or alteration to make an overall design, then it has to be scaled down to concentrate on whatever situation is under one's control. In this there is always scope for self expression to contrive what appeals most to one's aesthetic sensitivity. In making this the first objective, ways of developing it to the full will open up given an open, but determined mind. It would be far more likely to succeed than if a professional were employed. Self expression in such a matter cannot come by paying someone else a fee for planning what they would not have to live with and in which perhaps they would have no further interest.

It is possible to perceive some link between harmony in one's garden and within one's self, though not without some reservations. For example, someone might set out to achieve gardening harmony because of personal strife or inner disharmony. Then it could be a palliative or sublimation but it appears somehow to be the wrong way round. It would be much more likely that anyone who is fortunate enough to acquire peace of mind by coming to terms within themselves and with any disruptive outside factors, would be better able to express that kind of harmony in their garden. A mind in acute turmoil usually seeks more drastic outlets. And it would then take considerable effort of will and concentration to find solace in the beauty of plants, or the art of caring for them.

In times past, I have sought relief for mental stress by slogging, with a hoe, spade, fork or scythe. Such physical exertion, with a survey of work done, coming with bodily fatigue, has almost invariably led to a better night's sleep and a clearer vision with a quieter mind by morning, along with new resolves. I have to admit that when sometimes stress became severe, both my mind and body tended to seize up for a day or two, making me slink into sheer, isolated indolence, but ending with a renewed if grim determination. Such occasions were rare, and apart from them I have always been thankful for having interesting and worthwhile outlets for energy. And it is with this in mind that I now see my choice of a profession as being suited to my somewhat cross-grained nature.

It is true that I have tended to bite off on many occasions more than I could chew and digest in comfort. But now, on the threshold of old age, I still prefer to be pushed for time rather than to have to look around for something to do. Always to have jobs waiting to be done brings a certain irony when there is not much sand left in the top half of the hour glass. The more enjoyable and interesting the work, the more swiftly time flies.

As a schoolboy time dragged horribly; as a young man, time ahead seemed endless, but with only a little to come, it races past. And the only compensation lies in reflecting again on my choice, for had I no useful, interesting work, needing to be done, which so many of my age lack, then there would be little to look forward to.

It is this looking forward which sustains devoted gardeners whatever their age. I can think of no occupation or pastime which can compare with it. Pastime, when dissected, is, however, a quite inappropriate term to apply to garden-minded folk. One does not tend plants merely to pass the time away, for in this there is a constant challenge. The greater the variety grown, the more absorbing this challenge becomes, accentuated by the changing stages of growth in keeping with the seasons. It is never a burdensome chore, nor can it become boring, for time passes slowly with boredom for company. One is apt to be impatient, to see something new or special come into flower, but because they refuse to be hurried, then a degree of patience becomes an acquired habit, just as the accumulation of knowledge about plants, bring a wisdom which calms the mind against misfortunes.

Which reminds me of the lady whose garden was devastated by spray drifting in from an adjoining farm field. It was June and she was so heartbroken that her husband said he would sue the farmer for damages. 'Don't,' she pleaded. 'It'll not be an antidote for the poison and will make an enemy of him. Ask him and his wife to come for drinks as friendly neighbours'. He came and was appalled at the damage, saying that there must have been a change of wind, having studied the weather conditions before sending his man to spray the field. 'Would it help', he added, 'if you replaced what's ruined and let me have the bill? And would you accept a load of manure to help them grow?'

I am also reminded of a neighbour's herd of cattle which broke out and caused considerable havoc in my garden one summer night, before trampling over beds of alpines in the nursery. The law would have been on our side, but there would have been bad feeling generated in assessing the damage, and a verdict in our favour would not in the end restore the plants or good neighbourly relations.

I have indulged in a few battles in my time. Not against a neighbour since the very early days, which ended in an uneasy stalemate until I saw the futility of it and gave in. Most battles were against authority, which I saw as matters of principle and justified grievance. Some I won and some I lost – one of each being already recounted. But age, and a little wisdom perhaps, have left me less ready to fight, and I am glad this streak of bellicosity has almost gone. I am much too content with the daily round and common task. But, if my two sons are up to their necks in the cares of running a business, it is as a result of their own choice. I used to warn them against the snags of expansion – with the old adage of 'making a rod for their own backs'. To some extent at least they might admit to this being true, and because of this repeat of my own experience I can feel sympathy when I know they are harassed. We live and learn – and I, too, am still learning.

Index